For Jane, Elizabeth, Emily, Richard and Thomas

Contents

Introduction

Economics everywhere

When, in July 2007, two hedge funds run by the Wall Street investment bank Bear Stearns ran into difficulty, few could have guessed at the scale of the dramatic events that would follow. The funds, which had been worth $1.5 billion at the beginning of the year, were invested in financial products linked to what quickly became the notorious American subprime market. Subprime loans, to US households with impaired credit histories (the joke was that they were 'Ninja' borrowers, with no income, no job and no assets) had been around for many years. They however, along with adjustable rate mortgages (Arms), had expanded very rapidly from around 2003 and, more significantly, had been used as the basis for financial instruments – structured investment vehicles – sold to investors and traded between the banks. Mortgage-backed securities, as their name suggests, are financial instruments based on household mortgages. Even more sophisticated instruments, so-called credit derivatives based on those securities, 'sliced and diced' the original securities up even further and greatly multiplied the potential losses if there were problems with the underlying asset, the mortgage. The upshot was that if enough poor American families in Cleveland, Detroit or Fort Myers fell behind with their payments or defaulted on their mortgages the consequences would be felt by investors and banks many thousands of miles away. Think of it as an inverted pyramid resting on the unstable foundations of risky mortgages.

The Bear Stearns hedge funds were, to risk mixing metaphors, the tip of a very large iceberg, an early warning of the problems that were to follow. Even in early August 2007 after American Home Mortgage had filed for bankruptcy, most experts dismissed talk of a global financial crisis and it seemed that the problems arising from America's subprime problems would be limited. However, it became clear that an international crisis was brewing when on 9 August the French bank BNP Paribas suspended three of its investment funds because of losses related to the US subprime market. An alarmed European Central Bank responded by pumping tens of billions of euros into Europe's money markets.

What followed was a kind of domino effect, with banks regarded as weak or excessively dependent on wholesale money markets – rather than savers' deposits – most heavily exposed. On 13 September, 2007 it was revealed that Northern Rock, Britain's fifth largest mortgage lender, was being supported by 'lender of last resort' assistance from the Bank of England. The following day saw the first run on a British bank since Overend & Gurney in 1866. (Northern Rock was eventually nationalised by Britain's Labour government, after a five-month attempt to find a viable private-sector buyer.)

After the excitement of August and September, when money markets froze from a lack of confidence between the banks in each other, there were hopes that the worst might be over. It was, however, a vain hope. In March 2008, after months in which Wall Street investment banks and America's other large banks had announced ever-larger write-downs and losses on their subprime-related investments, Bear Stearns was forced to sell itself at a knockdown price to competitor J. P. Morgan. The deal was only possible because it was accompanied by a $30 billion loan from the Federal Reserve, America's central bank. Bear Stearns, founded in 1923, had been part of Wall Street's aristocracy, surviving the infamous crash of 1929 but now unable to weather the credit crunch of 2007–8. Indeed, the problems at its hedge funds eight months earlier had first exposed the crunch; now it was a victim of it. Soon afterwards, the International Monetary Fund said that the world was facing the biggest financial shock since the Great Depression of the 1930s.

Economic history in the making
Comparisons with the Great Depression and the bank runs of the Victorian era provided confirmation that something highly unusual was happening in the global economy. Indeed, policy-makers looked to Walter Bagehot, the nineteenth-century

economist, social theorist and constitutional reformer, who was editor of *The Economist* during the run on Overend & Gurney in the 1860s. Apart from computer technology, the global nature of the crisis and the fact that every move was played out on twenty-four-hour television, very little appeared to have changed since Bagehot's day. 'Every great crisis reveals the excessive speculations of many houses which no one before suspected,' he wrote in *Lombard Street: A Description of the Money Market*, published in 1873. And, 'the good times too of high price almost always engender much fraud. There is a happy opportunity for ingenious mendacity. Almost everything will be believed for a little while, and long before discovery the worst and most adroit deceivers are geographically and legally beyond the reach of punishment.' Bagehot also understood what engendered financial panics: 'Any notion that money is not to be had, or that it may not be had at any price, only raises alarm to panic and enhances panic to madness.' As for the way such panics could envelop even those regarding themselves as too good, or too big to fail he comments: 'A panic grows by what it feeds on; if it devours these second-class men shall we, the first-class, be safe?'

People turned to history for the answers because the events of 2007–8 were so unusual in the modern era. What, for example, was a credit crunch? Defined as a sudden reduction in the availability of credit and an increase in its price, this was a modern-day rarity. Recent history is littered with examples of governments or central banks deliberately restricting the flow of credit to the economy and increasing interest rates. For such a phenomenon to occur 'naturally' as a result of a sudden collapse of confidence in the banking and financial system was, however, different. It resulted, for example, in a 70 per cent downward slide over twelve months in mortgage approvals – the number of new loans being granted – in Britain. The consequence of that extreme mortgage rationing was a dramatic drop in house prices. The discussion of Britain's housing market and the debate over prices in Chapter Two of this book does not, you will see, even consider this possibility. While interest rates can and do rise and fall, the idea of a sudden turning off of the credit taps did not come into the debate. This was, if not uncharted territory, outside the direct experience of policymakers. The ready availability of credit had almost come to be regarded as the economic equivalent of oxygen or running water.

As comparisons with the Great Depression were made by the IMF and others, economists scurried for their reference works. J. K. Galbraith's *The Great Crash, 1929* first published in the 1950s, jumped back into the bestseller lists. Ben Bernanke, chairman of the Federal Reserve in succession to Alan Greenspan, suddenly appeared to be in the right place at the right time, as one of the foremost academic authorities on Depression-era economics. He had always argued that understanding the Depression was the most important challenge for economists, if only to prevent history from repeating itself. Mention of the Depression also brought John Maynard Keynes, who gets a chapter to himself in this book (Chapter Ten), to the fore.

A Drama and a Crisis

During September and much of October, 2008, it seemed that

each weekend brought a new crisis that threatened to bring the financial system to its knees. The crisis that had begun more than a year earlier entered a new and more deadly phase. Suddenly, the fear of losses and counterparty risks (banks and other institutions not trusting counterparts they had previously been comfortable dealing with) reached exaggerated levels. For investment banks in particular, reliant on raising funds in the wholesale markets – unlike commercial banks they lacked retail customers – this lack of confidence was dangerous in the extreme. The drama began on the weekend of 6 September with an announcement from the US Treasury of a taxpayer-funded bailout of Fannie Mae (the Federal National Mortgage Association) and Freddie Mac (the Federal Home Loan Corporation), the bulwarks of America's mortgage market. Though owned by shareholders, both Fannie Mae and Freddie Mac are so-called government sponsored enterprises, with access to lower cost funds than commercial rivals and chartered by Congress to increase home ownership. The fact that they had to be rescued was testimony to the scale of the problem.

But, it was the non-rescue the following weekend, of the blue-blooded Wall Street investment bank Lehman Brothers, that really sent financial markets into a spin, almost producing, what for once it was not an exaggeration to call, 'financial meltdown'. A few weeks later Mervyn King, the Governor of the Bank of England, described the recent events:

Since August 2007, the industrialised world has been engulfed by financial turmoil. And, following the failure of Lehman Brothers on 15 September, an extraordinary, almost unimaginable, sequence of events began which culminated a week or so ago in the announcements around the world of a recapitalisation of the banking system. It is difficult to exaggerate the severity and importance of those events. Not since the beginning of the First World War has our banking system been so close to collapse. In the second half of September, companies and non-bank financial institutions accelerated their withdrawal from even short-term funding of banks, and banks increasingly lost confidence in the safety of lending to each other. Funding costs rose sharply and for many institutions it was possible to borrow only overnight. Credit to the real economy almost stopped flowing.

The 'almost unimaginable' sequence of events described by King included a $700 billion bailout of the US banking system by America's Treasury Department, a plan only approved after a tough battle with Congress. Even that failed to calm fevered markets. In Britain it included the nationalisation of much of Bradford & Bingley, a mortgage bank, and the emergency merger of Lloyds TSB and Halifax Bank of Scotland (HBOS) with the government waiving competition rules to allow the deal through. Banks were in trouble, and had to be rescued. Merrill Lynch, another Wall Street giant, was forced into a merger with Bank of America. AIG, America's biggest insurer, had to be rescued by the US government. Several European banks, including the Belgian–Dutch Fortis Bank and Germany's Hypo Real Estate Bank, got into trouble. The contagion was spreading dangerously and no institution appeared to be safe.

In the 1930s, operating on the principle that it was some-times necessary to save capitalism from itself, Keynes had urged government intervention. When markets and economies fail, he had argued, it was necessary for the state to act. This philos-ophy, often thought of as a desire for 'big' government, was nothing of the sort. 'The important thing for Government is not to do things which individuals are doing already, and to do them a little better or a little worse, but to do those things which at present are not done at all,' he wrote in *The End of Laissez-Faire*. In 2008 investors were not prepared to provide undercapitalised banks with the cash injections they needed. Liquidity was scarce in the money markets and so was trust. So governments had to do what Keynes said they should in such circumstances; step in.

A British plan, championed by Prime Minister Gordon Brown, appeared to press all the right buttons of bank recapital-isation, government lending guarantees and liquidity. It included a £37 billion taxpayer-funded capital injection into Royal Bank of Scotland, Lloyds and HBOS. There were £250 billion of government guarantees of bank lending – dependent on banks accepting the need for either publicly or privately-funded addi-tional capital. The final element was a doubling from £100 bil-lion to £200 billion in the amount the Bank of England was prepared to pump into the system in liquidity. An exceptional crisis required exceptional measures, and other countries took similar actions. When you read this you will know how well, or badly, these rescue attempts worked.

There was more of Keynes, or his memory, in the crisis solutions offered. Britain and other governments attempted to increase elements of public spending to offset the recessionary impact of the credit crunch, this being Keynes's remedy in the 1930s. There was talk too of a new Bretton Woods conference to establish a new framework for the global financial system; echoing the 1944 conference Keynes had dominated with his presence. Keynes, it seemed, was back.

*
**

The financial crisis of 2007–8 took economists, politicians and business people by surprise. Though many claimed with hindsight to have spotted it coming, few did. Out of a clear blue sky a financial hurricane blew, with damaging economic consequences. Some will say it showed the limitations of economics, but while economists engage in forecasting, they are not psychics or soothsayers. And, in an important sense, the crisis was when economics came into its own. As this brief introduction has tried to show, policymakers looked to the past for solutions to the difficult economic present. If the economy did the same thing, year-in, year-out, economics would be boring and few would look to economists for solutions. It is when things are exciting, even frightening, that economics comes alive. I hope this book will whet your appetite to delve further into the subject.

London, October 2008

Appetizer

This is a book about economics. I realize by writing that I risk losing about half of the bookshop browsers who have picked it up in the hope of coming across something interesting. But hold on. This is also a book about economics quite unlike any other. There are no tricky diagrams of the kind that leaves you wondering whether the page has been printed the right way up. There are no complicated mathematical equations. Unless something can be easily explained, it has no place here. Above all, at a time when we all need to know some economics, it is intensely practical. It will not necessarily make you a millionaire – I always say that the only economists you see driving Rolls-Royces are wearing chauffeurs' caps – but it will tell you about the process by which we become, mainly, better off. It is also, I hope, good fun.

The aim of this book is to fill a gap, just like a good lunch. For years, at the *Sunday Times* and elsewhere, readers have been asking me to recommend an easily digestible book on economics, either for non-economists or for those whose grasp of it is a little rusty. Until now I have found it difficult to do so. There are some excellent textbooks on economics, some of which I shall recommend later, but they are intended for formal courses of study, with teachers offering a guiding hand. This is different. I hope that many students will read and profit from *Free Lunch* but in a way that complements formal study rather than replaces it. There are, too, some excellent works describing recent economic history but these can be difficult, if not impossible, in the absence of the building blocks. An account of, say, Alan Greenspan's time as Chairman of the Federal Reserve Board in Washington needs the context of knowing something about monetary policy and how central banks are supposed to operate it. Similarly, trying to judge whether an assessment of the success of Tony Blair and Gordon Brown's management of the economy is fair or not requires a few basic tools.

Why have I called it *Free Lunch*? It is not, whatever you might think, a sneaky attempt to increase sales by passing off a work on economics as an addition to the ever-popular and expanding catalogue of cookbooks, although that would not be a bad idea. Rather, it is because the one snappy phrase from economics most people will have heard of, even if they are unaware it has anything to do with the subject, is: 'There's no such thing as a free lunch.' You never, in other words, get something for nothing. As I am a journalist often required to lunch, not always enjoyably, it has always been close to my heart. It is such a famous phrase, incidentally, that its origins are unclear. While it is often attributed to the American economist Milton Friedman, of whom more later, the *Oxford Dictionary of Quotations* lists its authorship as Anonymous, first coming into circulation in American university economic departments in the 1960s but making it into print, not in a textbook or learned article, but in *The Moon is a Harsh Mistress*, a 1966 novel by the science-fiction writer Robert Heinlein. It is likely, however, that the phrase was in use much earlier than this. The *San Francisco News* used it in a 1949 editorial, itself reputed to be a reprint of one written in 1938, while the legendary New York mayor Fiorello La Guardia said it in 1934, albeit in Latin. As for the origin of the idea, bars in the west of America commonly offered free lunch to patrons buying a certain amount of alcohol. Those who stayed sober soon worked out that they were paying for their lunch with what they were being charged for beer or whisky.

Does 'There's no such thing as a free lunch' work as a piece of economics? Most of us can think of cases where we have apparently got something for nothing. That bus fare you did not pay, or that £10 note you picked up on the street, for example. But think about it. The free fare has a cost, not just in the risk of prosecution but also in that fare-dodgers mean, in the long run, higher fares for all, including you. As for that windfall £10, I would not pretend that there is some higher economic authority guaranteeing that everybody's lucky gains and losses even out exactly over time but it is likely that something approximating to that is close to most people's experience. Any gambler will tell you how hard it is, over time, to stay ahead of the bookmaker; any stock market investor that it is difficult to beat the index consistently.

Let me give you another example of the 'free lunch' idea at work. If you have just bought this book, thanks, and you have proved that there is, indeed, no such thing as a free lunch. If you have borrowed it from a friend, you are obliged to them, and your payment will probably be to have to lend them something of yours. If it is from a library, you are paying for it in taxes, or will eventually do so. And if you have stolen it, then shame on you, but you are paying for it with a guilty conscience and you might get caught. My contract with you is that, in return for obtaining this book, by the time you've read it, you will know as much economics as you will probably ever need and more than the vast majority of the population. Except, of course, in the unlikely event that everybody else reads it too. That would put me in a monopoly position, although not for long, because economics tells us that we would then see a flood of entrants into the market from similar works. Economics could become the new cookery.

At one level the book is an aid to reading newspapers, particularly the financial pages, and understanding (and being able to see through) the economic claims and counter-claims of politicians. Why are we interested in inflation, the level of interest rates, the balance of payments and the budget deficit, and what do they really mean? Why are we interested in some of these things more than others, and at certain times rather than others? No longer when you see economic stories on the financial pages (and increasingly the front pages) should your reaction be to turn over. The only newspaper or magazine economic reports that should be hard to understand are those that are badly written. When you hear a politician saying that this year his government is spending a record amount on the health service you will be able to scream at the TV, as I do: 'But that's been the case virtually every year since the National Health Service was created!' Every voter should know some economics.

There is, however, more to *Free Lunch* than that. When I urge school or college audiences to study economics, it is not just because some such knowledge is essential for modern living. Rather, it is because the way that economists think about and analyse problems in a logical way is useful in so many areas. Watching economists at work is not always a pretty sight and the jokes about their indecisiveness are legion. President Harry Truman yearned for a one-handed economist because every one that he knew said: 'On the one hand this, on the other hand that.' You could, according to the hoary saying, lay every economist in the world end to end and never reach a conclusion. This is unfair, confusing the invaluable ability of economists to be able to see the other side of the argument with an apparent inability to reach decisions. Thinking like an economist means approaching problems in a logical manner, replacing assertion with analysis. This book will not turn you into a professional economist overnight but it will encourage you to think differently about things.

Free Lunch, like all good meals, comes in several courses. It can be digested at a single sitting, taken a course at a time or, if you like, dipped into from time to time for a snack. I hope very much that you enjoy it.

2

Starters

Many books on economics begin by saying something like: 'Economics is about the allocation of scarce resources between competing demands.' Or, according to a very good and widely used textbook: 'Economics is the study of how society decides what, how and for whom to produce.' These are splendid definitions and undoubtedly correct as far as they go but they suffer from two important drawbacks. The first is that it is not until you have studied quite a lot of economics that you really understand what they mean. The second is that they are, for me, just too limited. Economics dominates and shapes our daily lives, even when we are not aware of it. It is all encompassing. This does not mean we exist only as economic men and women, or are obsessed by money. It does mean that there is no getting away from economics. We refer, after all, to countries as 'economies'. I like the definition used by the great Eng-

lish economist Alfred Marshall (1842–1924) who said economics was the study of people 'in the ordinary business of life'.

Much of it also comes back to food, which is why I like the
title of this book. Anne Sibert, head of economics and statistics
at Birkbeck College, London, uses a restaurant analogy to
explain how speculative frenzies – financial bubbles – build up in
the stock market. There are two restaurants in a town, the Ritz
and the Savoy. Albert does not much mind which one he goes
to but chooses the Ritz. Ben, coming next, is leaning slightly
towards the Savoy but, seeing that Albert is at the Ritz, decides
that it must be better. Catherine is also persuaded by Albert and
Ben's choice that the Ritz must be the place, and so is David. By
the time we get halfway through the alphabet to Mary, everybody has chosen the Ritz and nobody the Savoy. But then
Neville, who is next, has a very strong preference for the Savoy,
partly because the Ritz is by now very crowded. Olivia, seeing
Neville's choice, follows him, so does Peter, and so do the rest,
right through to Zak. And then something strange happens.
Halfway through their meal, all those who chose the Ritz hear
that everybody else is going to the Savoy. They leave, in a rush,
to go from one to another, to the Ritz's chagrin. Think of all
those who initially chose the Ritz as people who invested in
dot.com shares a few years ago, and think of the rush to get out
as they realized that they had invested in worthless companies,
and you have a pretty good analogy for how bubbles build up
and are burst.

Anyway, this is holding things up. The waiter is hovering and
the meal is about to start. What shall we talk about? According

to journalistic folklore, the only thing the middle classes talk about when gathered together at dinner parties is house prices. Whether that is true or not, let us take it as our starting-point.

Houses versus potatoes

Most conversations about the housing market will include several elements. One person will assert that house prices have risen too much and are about to fall, while somebody else will claim that they have a lot further to rise. There is bound to be an argument over whether it is better to put your money into housing or stocks and shares. Everybody will count their good fortune to be already several rungs up the housing ladder and not a first-time buyer struggling to scrape together a deposit for a home. Home ownership was one of the great economic developments of the twentieth century. Roughly 70 per cent of people in Britain either own their home outright, or are buying it with the help of a mortgage. Canada, the United States and Australia have similar proportions. In Spain it is a little higher, nearer 80 per cent. In Germany it is somewhat lower, below 50 per cent, with home-buying usually occurring at a later age. Despite these differences, our obsession with the subject is understandable.

Unfortunately, as markets go, the one for housing is quite complicated. Imagine for a moment that the middle-class obsession was with the price of potatoes, which had risen to a very high level. Both the economist and the non-economist – the former after long years of study, the latter instinctively – would know how to analyse this. If the price of potatoes is very high, many people will decide they are spending too much of their income on them and switch to alternatives, such as rice and pasta, reducing potato demand. High prices discourage people from buying, while low prices encourage them. The effect on potato suppliers is, however, the opposite. High prices are an encouragement to supply more, while low prices act as a disincentive. Of course it may not be possible to conjure up extra supplies instantly, although these days the supermarket chains operate very long storage times for so-called fresh foods. One reason why the prices of fresh produce traditionally varied so much from season to season was because supply varied between glut and shortage, depending on weather conditions and the extent to which farmers had responded to price signals (for example, planting more in response to this year's high prices).

The point, returning to our dinner table conversation about potatoes, is that if their prices have risen very high compared with competing products, this is unlikely to last. Demand will fall, because other foods look relatively cheap. Supply will increase because it looks as if there is more profit to be made in potatoes. The net result will be lower prices. There's quite a lot of economics in all that but the only things to remember are, firstly, that whereas the higher the price, the lower in general the demand, the opposite is the case for supply. The second is that prices are determined by the interaction of supply and demand. In our example potato prices will fall by enough to make people want to buy more of them but not by enough to discourage suppliers from increasing their output. The price mechanism really is wonderful, ensuring that supply and demand match up, that the market achieves equilibrium, or balance. Markets tend

9

towards equilibrium, towards the balancing of supply and demand. Remember that and you are well on your way to understanding market economics.

Housing and 'lemons'

It would be a strange and rather sad meal if the guests sat around talking about potatoes, so let us return to house prices. Many people think that the unusual thing about housing, indeed, is the extent to which prices have risen over time. In the 1930s, while much of Britain was suffering in the Great Depression and prices for everything including houses were falling, a great building boom was under way in and around London, creating suburbia. New Ideal Homesteads sold three-bed semis in Sidcup, Kent, for £250, houses that would now cost you £150,000 to £200,000. Modern Homes sold rather grander properties in Pinner, Middlesex, for between £850 and £1,500. To buy one now would cost between £600,000 and £1m. These changes are dramatic but then plenty of things have increased in price over time. My first pint of beer (consumed at a very young age) cost the equivalent of 10 pence. Now it would be twenty times that or more. Inflation, the rise in the general price level, means that we look back with nostalgia at the prices we used to pay. All that has happened to house prices is that they have risen more rapidly than prices generally – they have outpaced inflation – and there is an explanation for that, which I shall come on to.

What is unusual about housing, a peculiarity it shares with only a few other things such as antiques, fine art and vintage wine, is that its price rises even as you own it. Housing, to economists, is not just something you 'consume' – it gives you warmth, shelter and a place to sleep – it is also an asset. Contrast what happens to house prices with other, apparently very solid, products. Most fall in price, either because they deteriorate with use or become obsolete. Try selling a ten-year-old computer. It is well known that if you buy a new car, it will usually be worth about 20 per cent less than you paid for it the moment you drive it out of the showroom. A famous article in 1970 by the economist George Akerlof, 'The Market for Lemons' – lemons in this case being American for 'dud' – explained why this was. In 2001 Akerlof was jointly awarded the Nobel Prize for economics. Any buyer being offered a nearly new car by its owner would immediately assume that there must be something wrong with it, that it is a lemon, and thus will not be prepared to pay anything like the full price for it. This applies even if the car is perfect. Only sellers really know whether a car is perfect or not, buyers can never really be certain. Economists call this 'asymmetry of information', but do not worry about the jargon. The effect, as Akerlof explained, was to drive down prices across the whole market. Buyers will tend to assume, unfairly perhaps, that all second-hand cars are 'lemons'. And as long as this is the case, sellers have little incentive to sell good quality second-hand cars. Interestingly, the big car manufacturers have made an explicit effort to correct this lemon effect in the market by offering extended warranties on new cars and special guarantees on the second-hand vehicles sold by their dealerships.

When we talk about the housing market, we are talking by and large about a second-hand market. New houses are built every year but their number is tiny, perhaps a 1 per cent increase in supply in relation to the existing housing stock. The net addition to that stock each year, taking into account properties removed from the market by demolition or conversion into offices, is even smaller. Why, if most houses are second-hand, do they not suffer from the lemon effect? Some, it should be said, do. In the winter of 2000–2001 many parts of Britain suffered their worst flooding for decades. One immediate consequence, experts said, would be that properties in areas prone to flooding would become more difficult to sell, or only sellable at significantly lower prices, because people willing to put up with flood risk would require some compensation for doing so. In the late 1980s, in response to strong demand, Britain's house-builders built thousands of tiny boxes and called them 'starter homes'. Like flood-prone houses later, these subsequently became hard to sell. They became lemons.

In general, though, second-hand houses do not suffer in this way. Even if they need money spent on them, as they usually do, and even if that involves more than what might have been revealed by the structural survey, which it usually does, buyers are not deterred, for two reasons. One is that, except in extreme circumstances, the cost of repairs and improvements usually represents only a small fraction of the cost (and therefore to the buyer the value) of the property. The second is that people are willing to spend money on their houses because they see this as maintaining or improving an asset that is going to go up in value. As an aside, a perennial debate in the property pages is whether you ever get back, in the eventual selling price of the house, what you have spent on double-glazing, a conservatory or a kitchen. In other words, does your house sell for a sufficient amount more than the unimproved property down the road? To an economist, that may be a sensible question for a property developer to ask himself, but it does not have a lot of relevance to the ordinary homeowner. This is because the gains from any improvements fall into two categories – the 'consumption' of those improvements in the form of more warmth, comfort or space, and the effect on the value of the property. Splitting the two is very difficult indeed, not least because it will vary according to individual preferences.

While we are at it, let us nail another newspaper (and dinner party) favourite. Can you compare the rise in the price of your house and that of investments in the stock market? The answer is no, unless you have a way of valuing the non-financial benefits – warmth, shelter and so on – you have received from housing along the way, which share certificates do not offer. Not only that but, on the other side, most people do not take out a mortgage to buy stocks and shares (although they do forgo the interest they could have obtained from putting their cash in a deposit account). It is a case, though I hesitate to introduce more fresh produce into the discussion, of comparing apples and pears. Even for developers, the calculation is not easy. Most measures of long-run stock market performance assume that share dividends are not taken as income but reinvested. The equivalent for a landlord would be that rental income was immediately invested in additional properties, and the comparison would then be between the rise in the value of an entire property portfolio, not any single house, and that of the stock market.

We have got this far without addressing a rather important question. People are prepared to spend money on their houses, not just because they want to live in more comfortable and spacious surroundings, but also because they think they are investing in an appreciating asset. History tells us that they are right to think that but it does not explain why.

Why house prices rise

One of the most enduring economic relationships is that between house prices and people's incomes. House prices rise because incomes do. The house price/earnings ratio – the ratio of average house prices to national average earnings for full-time workers – is around 3.5 over the long run, usually fluctuating between three and four. If average earnings are £20,000 a year – they are actually a little bit above that at the time of writing – average house prices will be around £70,000. It is easy to see why this relationship should exist. Suppose house prices had not risen and were stuck at their 1930s level. Someone on average earnings could buy several houses in the London suburbs a year, instead of buying one and paying for it over the twenty-five years of a mortgage. We are back to supply and demand. In this case rising demand does not mean that everybody wants to own a string of houses. It does mean the amount they can afford to pay for their semi has increased hugely and, more importantly, so has the amount others can afford to pay. Competition among buyers, all of whom have been able to pay more over time, pulls house prices higher.

Rising incomes pull house prices higher and incomes have risen steadily, and by about 2 per cent a year more than inflation (in other words in 'real' terms) for as long as anybody can remember. If we go back forty years, average earnings were a few hundred pounds a year. They have risen twenty-five-fold while prices have increased fifteen-fold. Certain groups of workers, of course, do better than others. I am old enough to remember the first £100-a-week professional footballer. Now the top-paid players get nearly £100,000 a week. I shall return later to the reasons why earnings usually rise faster than prices. One entertaining way of demonstrating that they do is by reference to the time an average person has to work to earn enough to afford certain products. Thus, in 1900 the average worker had to toil for a couple of hours to earn enough to buy a loaf of bread. Today it is about five minutes.

There is also an institutional element in the relationship between house prices and incomes. Banks and building societies base their mortgage-lending decisions on the income, and therefore ability to pay, of the borrower, offering an advance that is a multiple of annual salary. That multiple can be as high as four, five or six times the salary, although the average is only just over two. Interestingly, the ratio of house prices to incomes is usually significantly higher for older people, who have been homeowners longer, than for first-time buyers. This is because, while for first-time buyers the mortgage covers a high proportion of the value of the property, longer-term homeowners have usually built up capital, or 'equity', in their house. Someone buying a £25,000 house on a £20,000 mortgage has £5,000 of equity. If the value of the house rises to £100,000, the amount of equity increases to £80,000. There is, incidentally, little evidence that the housing market has become progressively more difficult for first-time buyers to enter, particularly when the level of interest rates is taken into account, of which more below. Indeed, the opposite may be true. In the past – until the early 1980s – when mortgage lending was limited to the building societies and rationing was common (societies had to have enough income from savers to lend out in mortgages), entering the market was a long and tortuous process.

I said the housing market is different. Why, as in our potato example, do house-builders not respond to high prices by flooding the market with new houses? And why does this not bring prices down, as it would for other products? The answer is that new houses account each year for only a tiny proportion of the existing housing stock. Land, to go back to some of those definitions at the start of this chapter, is a scarce resource. And planners ensure that, as far as building is concerned, it remains so. If there were no planning restrictions and any farmer could sell a few fields for housebuilding, the housing market would be more like the market for potatoes. Big increases in supply would, from time to time, be followed by significant price falls. The planners, by preventing this from happening, help ensure rising house prices. The year 2000 was, on the face of it, a strong one for the housing market, with prices rising quite markedly and mortgage demand buoyant. It was a weak one, however, for housebuilding, which dropped to its lowest level since 1924, the industry blaming planning rules intended to prevent development of greenfield sites. Housebuilding fell even further in 2001. It is possible to stretch available living space a little, by converting houses into flats, or offices and former factories into fashionable lofts. But the general point still holds. New supply is very small in relation to the size of the market. To economists supply is 'inelastic' – it responds only slowly to rising prices – whereas if builders were able to flood the market with new properties in response to high prices it would be 'elastic'.

Two prices for housing

We have got this far without touching on something rather important as far as housing is concerned, and there is just time to talk about it before the next course. When people talk about their house, they usually know how much they paid for it. They usually have a rough (sometimes a very precise) idea of how much it is worth. But, as every homeowner knows, as important as the price is the monthly mortgage outlay and that, in turn, depends on the level of interest rates. An easy way of demonstrating this is as follows. Suppose I buy a house for £100,000, on a full repayment mortgage, and pay for it over twenty-five years at an average interest rate of 10 per cent, the total cost to me in monthly payments over the period is £275,418. If, on the other hand, the average interest rate were 5 per cent, repayments over twenty-five years would be £177,381. The difference is nearly as much as the original price of the house. Before anybody jumps up and down, £100,000 now is clearly worth more than £100,000 spread over twenty-five years. Newspaper competitions sometimes offer choices of prize money in the form of either a large amount upfront or a somewhat smaller amount paid weekly for life. There are few takers for the latter. The economic principle behind this is similar to the old proverb: 'A bird in the hand is worth two in the bush.'

Suppose you had the choice between £100,000 now or £200,000 spread over twenty-five years, which would you take? Before you opened this book your instinct may have been to go for the larger sum. Armed with some economics, however, the kind of calculation you would make would focus on the rate of interest you could earn on that money over the period. At a 4 per cent interest rate, which is quite low, £100,000 invested now would rise to £200,000 in fifteen years. At a rate of just over 2.5 per cent – and UK interest rates have not been that low since just after the Second World War – it would double over twenty-five years. Put another way, if you were asked what £200,000 spread over twenty-five years was worth to you now, the answer might be, depending on what you expect interest rates to do, a much smaller sum, perhaps £40,000 or £60,000. This is known in economics as the present value of a sum received in the future. The number you have used to come up with it is called the discount factor – how much you would be prepared to trade money upfront for a stream of income in the future. It is most commonly used in decisions about investment. In this case it tells us that to match the offer of £100,000 now, something rather more than £200,000 would have to be offered spread over twenty-five years.

I have digressed again, and time is moving on. The central point is that while the initial price of a house will be the main factor in the amount of a mortgage, the level of interest rates determines how much that mortgage costs. This is where analysis of the housing market gets quite interesting. Many amateur observers of the market, and quite a few professionals, have a blind spot when it comes to this. A fierce debate raged in Britain in 2001–2 about whether a housing 'boom' then under way was about to come to a sticky end, as its predecessor did in the early 1990s. A little nervousness was perhaps in order. Peaking in 1989, house prices fell by between 20 and 30 per cent over the next four years, and by much more in some areas. Those who had bought near the top, and quite a few more, found themselves in 'negative equity' where the value of their property was less, by a considerable amount in some cases, than the mortgage they had taken out to buy it. This, the opposite of the equity enjoyed by most homeowners in their houses, affected more than a million households. A fall in house prices of this kind had not happened in Britain since the general deflation (a period of falling prices for everything) of the 1930s.

As in 1989, said the worriers of 2001, the ratio of house prices to incomes had begun to stretch higher. Surely this presaged an imminent collapse? The trouble with this was that it ignored the crucial factor of interest rates. In 1989 interest rates rose to 15 per cent. In 2001 they dropped to 4 per cent. The implication, in terms of monthly mortgage outlays, was huge – people could afford to borrow more while using a smaller proportion of their income in payments. They could afford to 'gear' themselves up. Indeed, much of what was happening to the housing market at the turn of the millennium and after could be seen as a gradual adjustment from the high interest rates of the 1970s and 1980s to the much lower rates that prevailed from around 1993 onwards. There may be an argument for a permanent upward adjustment in the normal ratio between house prices and incomes.

One puzzle observers from other countries sometimes have is that mortgage rates are such a hot political issue in Britain. Gordon Brown's decision to give control of interest rates – independence – to the Bank of England in 1997 was partly to get away from the interview question that had dogged every Chancellor of the Exchequer: 'Are interest rates going up or down?' The reason it is a hot issue is that, traditionally, the vast majority of people with mortgages had variable-rate loans: every time the general level of interest rates changed, often monthly, so did their payments. This contrasted with other countries, where often the rate was fixed for the life of the mortgage. There has been a shift in recent years, with more new loans being on fixed rates of interest. But this has not rid the housing market of its interest-rate sensitivity. Apart from the fact that a large number of existing borrowers still have variable-rate mortgages, most fixed-rate loans are for relatively short periods, usually up to five years. And changes in short-term interest rates affect the rate on fixed-rate loans offered to new borrowers.

This is not to say other countries have not had housing market problems. Both Germany and Japan have had falling house prices since the early 1990s. In France, where flexibility of supply has tended to act as a dampener on house price rises, Britain's periodic property booms are seen as a peculiarly Anglo-Saxon phenomenon. The general point still holds. Sharply rising interest rates will tend to be associated with a weakening of housing demand, and vice versa when rates are falling.

Intelligent observations

Sorry to have gone on so much about housing. It just shows that when you get into a conversation about these things it can be hard to stop. What it also shows is that a little bit of economics can take you a long way. No longer do you have to wonder uneasily whether the pub bore might be right when he tells you that house prices are going to fall for the next thirty years. Just ask him whether he thinks incomes are going to fall over that period, and why that should be. No longer, too, do you have to smile politely when somebody suggests that, irrespective of the level of interest rates, house prices are too high. You know better. And when you see one of those newspaper pieces asking whether houses or shares are the better investment, either read it with a superior smile on your face or just turn the page. This is what economics is about, replacing assertion with argument, anecdote with analysis. And as we shall see, it can be applied to very many things 'in the ordinary business of life'.

Interest rates and incomes are vital to the housing market but we have not talked about what determines them. That will come soon. In economics, as most people know, the study of individual markets is known as 'microeconomics', while both interest rates and the growth of incomes are 'macroeconomic' variables – concerned with the overall economy. Micro is small, macro big. Housing is a bit unusual in that respect too. While economists would regard the market for potatoes or, say, the housing market in Milton Keynes, as the preserve of microeconomics, the housing market in aggregate is so important that it makes it into the macroeconomic arena. All will become clearer when we look at how economic policy works. Time, however, is moving on. A sip of wine, and then on to the main course.

3

Main course (1)

Rude of me, I know, but I have not yet introduced you to the other guests at the table. Meet Mr and Mrs Rational – economic man and economic woman. They are not a bad couple, even if everything they do can be a bit predictable. I shall come on to them in a moment but let me just set out the aim of this main course. It is easy to get the idea that economics is about the billions of dollars flowing around the world's financial markets, or about whether the Chancellor increases public spending or taxes by a billion pounds or two, but human behaviour is at the heart of it. The aim, then, is to start with the behaviour of economic man and woman and try to build up from that to a picture of how the economy as a whole works. If that sounds a bit daunting, let me assure you it will not be. We will just start at the bottom and work our way up. Time to tuck in.

Behaving economically

Many people have trouble with the idea that human behaviour is predictable. Surely, most will say, it is inherently unpredictable. Economic man or woman may be acceptable in the textbooks but do they really exist in real life? If you are like me there are plenty of times when you will have made a stupid purchase (one of the 'lemons' of the last chapter) or some other bad and apparently unfathomable economic decision. On a more mundane level, how can economics explain why I choose to buy a new shirt on a whim, or walk to work rather than catch the bus? An aerial view of Oxford Street would surely show us scurrying around haphazardly, like a colony of ants.

Apart from the fact that there is nothing haphazard about the way a colony of ants behaves, the essence of economics is that human behaviour follows predictable patterns. When the price of something falls, for example, we will tend to buy more. There is nothing difficult or surprising about that. Even so, it appears that many see it as pseudo-scientific mumbo jumbo. Denis Healey, Britain's Chancellor of the Exchequer from 1974 to 1979, perhaps one of the most torrid periods for the economy in modern times, found plenty to criticize in the economic advice he was given. He declared his intention of doing for economic forecasters 'what the Boston Strangler did for door-to-door salesmen – to make them distrusted for ever'. As for economics in general, he was far from convinced of its usefulness. He wrote in his autobiography, *The Time of My Life*: 'I decided that while economic theory can give you valuable insights into what is happening, it can rarely offer clear prescriptions for government action, since economic behaviour can change from year to year and is different in one country from another.'

Healey was not being as damning as he thought. His central point that behaviour can change from one year to the next and differs between countries is not one that any economist would have any difficulty with. During the period he was in charge inflation rose to a peak of more than 26 per cent, the stock market plunged by two-thirds in value, the world economy had to try to cope with a quadrupling of the price of oil and Britain, apparently on the brink of bankruptcy (although countries never actually go bankrupt) had to seek help from the International Monetary Fund. What was changing was not so much fundamental economic behaviour as the forces acting on that behaviour, which were outside previous experience. There is another point, and it is one we shall return to, which is that rational behaviour can mean behaving differently at different times in response to similar circumstances. If you have bought a dud timeshare holiday once, you probably would not do so again, even if faced with the same inducements. If the price of oil quadrupled again, you would want to take your money out of the stock market. This kind of learning process is part of rational economic behaviour.

What about that unpredictability point? How can anybody explain or predict why on a given day I decided, perhaps with this meal in mind, my wardrobe would not be complete without a purple and green striped shirt? What if everybody decided to buy one of those shirts on a particular day and then nobody decided to buy any shirts for a week? The answer is that, as long as there are enough of us, the unpredictable behaviour by some will cancel out. Even on an individual basis, we are not as unpredictable as you might think. An economist may not be able to predict the exact day you will buy that shirt, and he may not be able to explain your appalling taste in colours (although he could go a long way towards doing so). But he knows, given your income, you will buy a certain number of shirts over a period. That is why firms spend so much acquiring information on people's spending patterns and bombarding us with marketing literature that taps into those patterns. If everybody behaved haphazardly there would be no point in doing so.

Carrots and sticks

In his excellent book *The Armchair Economist*, Steven Landsburg writes: 'Most of economics can be summarised in four words: "People respond to incentives." The rest is commentary.' We have been here a little bit before, in the discussion in the last chapter on potatoes, and why they are different from houses. When potatoes fall in price we are likely to buy more of them and vice versa. Just to add to the confusion, incentives are popularly known as carrots and disincentives as sticks. Why do most of us keep working when there are much more pleasant things to do? Because the carrot of a gradually rising income bobs gently in front of our nose, while the stick of an alternative life of destitution brings up the rear.

The most obvious example of incentives is the one already described. When the price of something falls we will tend to buy more of it. There are exceptions to this rule but not many. A few years ago, when a price war broke out between newspapers in Britain, many economists thought that newspaper proprietors were effectively throwing money away because people did not buy papers on price. Because the cost of a paper represented such a low proportion of income, a little like the usual textbook example of a box of matches, demand was expected to be unresponsive to changes in price, or 'inelastic'. In fact, it turned out to be quite elastic, demand for *The Times* increasing in response to price cuts, with the overall broadsheet market expanding when other newspapers followed suit. Economists are always looking for exceptions to the rule. In the nineteenth century Robert Giffen noticed that for certain basic commodities, such as bread and potatoes, demand appeared to go up when prices rose. In very special circumstances, it worked. Imagine a family on very low incomes with a diet of potatoes and meat. When the price of potatoes goes up – but is still well below that for meat – their response is to cut out some of the meat and replace it with a larger amount of potatoes. Higher prices mean more, not less, demand. There may have been a real-life example of this during the Irish potato famine. Giffen's observation earned him a place in the economics equivalent of the Hall of Fame, with certain goods being known as Giffen goods. Economists have, however, found it hard to identify sustained examples of them. It is a curiosity rather than a rule.

So-called inferior goods can also break the normal rule. Tripe, cow's stomach, used to be part of the regular meat diet of many people, particularly those on modest incomes, in the Midlands and North. As people's incomes rose and the relative price of other meats fell, they were able to move on to chops, joints and even steaks. It did not matter that the price of tripe was falling, because demand also fell. These things, it should be said, can come full circle. Later, when French cuisine came to Britain in a big way, tripe became a delicacy much in demand at the best restaurants. It may even be on our menu today. Again, though, we should not get hung up about this. While it may have been true that over time the demand for tripe fell in spite of lower prices, on any given day during that process a butcher cutting his price could expect to sell more. You have to distinguish the short- and long-run effects.

Fish and chips

Paul Krugman, the American economist who is always worth reading, has a good example on his website of the effects of changing tastes and incomes. His short paper, 'Supply, Demand and English Food', tries to answer the question of why restaurant food in Britain, which 'used to be deservedly famous for its awfulness – greasy fish and chips, gelatinous pork pies and dishwater coffee', had suddenly got better. His conclusion was that industrialization and the shift of huge numbers of people from the country to towns and cities had made people in Britain forget about wholesome food and accept inferior, processed alternatives – canned vegetables and preserved meats – which were easier to ship and store. Prosperity rose but tastes did not change, mostly because people knew no better. According to Krugman, who is only half joking: 'Because your typical Englishman circa, say, 1975, had never had a really good meal, he didn't demand one.'

Only when people began to travel more widely, and began to experience other countries' cuisines, did they demand better quality. 'So what does all this have to do with economics?' asks Krugman.

> *Well, the whole point of a market system is supposed to be that it serves consumers, providing us with what we want and thereby maximising our collective welfare. But the history of English food suggests that, even on so basic a matter as eating, a free market economy can get trapped for an extended period in a bad equilibrium in which good things are not demanded because they have never been supplied, and are not supplied because not enough people demand them.*

Fun, and surely right.

Pricing to sell

Having wandered off down a little byway it is worth returning for a moment to the central point. Why do we buy more of something when its price falls? With the exception of Bill Gates and a fairly limited number of other very rich people, most of us are limited in what we can spend by our income; we are subject to a budget constraint. Within that constraint, we allocate our spending on the basis of necessity and desire – some on food, drink, travel, books, entertainment, and so on. I buy a certain number of CDs every year. I could buy more if I chose to eat a little less but I am happy with the way things are. I have made my choices. To economists, I am 'indifferent' between the number of CDs I buy and the number of meals I eat. Odd word, I know, but all it means is that, for a given level of income and pattern of prices, this combination of spending is right for me.

Now what would happen if the price of CDs were to halve? At the very least you might think that I would buy twice as many, because I could do so while devoting the same proportion of income to their purchase. I could, though, buy exactly the same number and use the money released to buy nicer meals, travel more or go to the cinema more often. I could even save more. If I did that, the cut in prices would have had no effect and our rule would have been broken. So what would one expect? Within my own pattern of spending, CDs have suddenly become cheap relative to everything else. The cost of other things, expressed in terms of CDs, has gone up. So my future desired pattern of spending will be for a higher proportion of CDs relative to other things. Economists call this the 'substitution' effect – shifting spending patterns in favour of things that have fallen in price or, in the opposite situation of a rise in prices, away from products that have gone up. We demonstrate the substitution effect every time we buy more of an item emblazoned with special offer signs at the supermarket.

There is also, however, another effect. The halving of the price of CDs has made me better off. Why? Before the price cut my income allowed me to buy food, housing, clothing, travel, and so on, plus about twenty CDs a year. Now that same income allows me all those things plus forty CDs. The fall in price is equivalent to an increase in my income. In that respect, it is like any other increase in income, so just as I would not spend all of a pay rise buying more CDs, neither will I in this case. This is known, unsurprisingly, as the 'income effect'. What it means, for me at least, is that the most likely result of a halving of the price of CDs will be quite a big increase in purchases of them (but not a doubling) and smaller increases in my consumption of everything else. In the opposite situation of a rise in the price of CDs, assuming no change in my income, all of the above would be reversed.

A good real-world example of this goes back to the previous chapter. When interest rates fall, one of the prices (and the costs) of housing – the one that affects household budgets – has come down. The substitution effect of this is that you think of buying a bigger house, and some people do so. The income effect is that you have become better off, a fall in interest rates being equivalent to a rise in the borrower's income. And, because you are better off, you spend more on items other than housing. That is one of the ways that monetary policy works, as we shall see later.

Getting satisfaction
Before moving on, time to tackle a little puzzle. What determines what we spend our money on? Why some things rather than others? Many people would answer 'need' to this question. Britain's Office for National Statistics, which produces the annual Family Expenditure Survey, on the basis of a sample of more than 7,000 households, found that at the end of the 1990s, for the first time, people were spending more on leisure than food. In 1999–2000 the average household spent £360 a week,

of which £62 was on leisure, £60 on food and non-alcoholic drink, £57 on housing (mortgage payments or rent), £53 on motoring, £31 on household goods, £21 on clothing, £19 on household services, £15 on alcohol, £14 on personal goods and services (such as hairdressing), £11 on fuel and power, £6 on tobacco, and so on. Earlier generations, of course, would not have had the luxury of devoting more than a sixth of their weekly spending to leisure, with feeding and housing the family taking up most, if not all, of their income. Prosperity has brought with it an increase in consumer choice. We can go to the opera (although a ticket at the Royal Opera House costs more than the average family's weekly leisure spend), or get fat on the sofa watching televised football. The other thing that determines how we spend our money is taste, our personal tastes.

Taking all the above as read, we still need to answer the question: why do we spend in the way we do? It may seem trivial but it was something that obsessed many of the great economists of the past, particularly in the nineteenth and early twentieth centuries. They were concerned with the satisfaction or 'utility' people obtained from consuming things. Some even believed it could be precisely measured. We need not trouble ourselves with that but utility is still a useful idea. In general, for example, the more of something we consume, the less satisfaction or utility we will get out of each extra one. One bar of chocolate a day is fine for me but a second I could take or leave. After a third I would feel queasy and after a fourth I would be quite ill. The amount of utility we get from each extra one, each 'marginal' one, falls. This is known as 'diminishing marginal utility' – the more you have the less you want another one. It can even go negative. After six cups of coffee in a morning, I would pay somebody to drink the seventh I was offered.

Diminishing marginal utility does not apply to everything. Collectors may get more satisfaction out of the final acquisition that completes a set than the first that began it. One harmless bit of fun economics opens up is thinking of exceptions to the rule. Are addicts, for example, subject to diminishing marginal utility?

Utility does allow us to answer some of the great mysteries of our time. Why, when there are so many wholesome alternatives around, do people buy and eat Pot Noodles, that well-known convenience food? Why don't students blow their entire loan in frenzied partying in the first week of term? Why do old men who drive cars in the middle of the road always wear trilby hats? Actually I cannot help with the third one (and if anybody can, let me know) but I can with the other two. It has to do with utility. What we all try to do, subconsciously – although I have met a few strange economists who do it consciously – is try to maximize our utility. In other words, we try to get the most out of what we spend. I would not be doing this if I spent my entire income on Mars bars, because diminishing marginal utility would kick in quite quickly. It may be that I could do it by alternating fillet steak with Pot Noodles. I suspect, however, that many aficionados of Pot Noodles maximize their utility by alternating them with copious quantities of beer in the student bar. As for why those same students do not blow their student loans in the first week, it is because it would not maximize their utility to have one glorious but soon forgotten binge and live on nothing for the rest of the year.

Incentives work everywhere

The idea that 'incentives work' underpins much of economics. It is also a basic tenet of economics that can be extended to other areas of life. Gary Becker, an American economist, won the Nobel Prize for economics in 1992 'for having extended the domain of microeconomic analysis to a wide range of human behaviour and interaction, including non-market behaviour'. Some of the ways incentives work are fairly obvious, if nevertheless controversial. How do you reduce the murder rate? By making the death sentence mandatory for all convicted murderers. I shall leave to you the question of whether this would, in turn, give juries an incentive not to convict. Crime and punishment are areas where the incentive model can be widely used. What is the best way of stopping people speeding in their cars? Is it to try to persuade them of the dangers of driving too fast or is it to install speed cameras on every stretch of road and slap heavy fines on transgressors? Current government policy in Britain, having tried the former for many years, now emphasizes the latter. Road safety is an area where incentives could be used more widely. Safe and conviction-free drivers already benefit from lower insurance premiums than their more dangerous counterparts. Why should not the government extend this incentive principle by varying rates of road tax depending on the safety record of the driver? Road safety is also an area, however, where incentives may operate in a perverse way. Do seat belts make people drive more carefully or, knowing that they are better protected in the event of a crash, more dangerously? Would the best way of ensuring safe driving be to require every vehicle to be fitted with a large spike in the centre of the steering wheel, as has been suggested, because nobody would then take any risks?

There are more entertaining examples of incentives. Why, in most western societies, is polygamy banned? On the surface it looks like a case of men, against their own self-interest, legislating in favour of women, ensuring they are not forced to share a husband. This assumes, however, that polygamy is a state desired by most men, which is debatable, since many would argue that one wife is plenty. It also ignores the fact that, in any society where there is a roughly equal number of men and women, polygamy will mean that, for every man with five or six wives there will be four or five sad and lonely ones without any wives at all. There is also the strong possibility that wives in a polygamous marriage will be less loyal, ready to respond to the blandishments of the richer chap down the road. Incentives work, and men can do without that kind of competition. Men have an incentive to outlaw polygamy. You can extend this to plenty of other areas. Were more liberal attitudes towards the position of women in the workforce driven by fairness, or by the desire of many men to be able to spend their afternoons on the sofa, watching the racing on television?

Steven Landsburg, in one of his regular pieces for *Slate*, the online magazine, offered another interesting angle on the role of incentives in society. Why, he asked, is there so much obesity around, particularly in America? The usual explanations revolve around the malign influences of TV, cars and fast food (including the defining moment when the standard unit of consumption for teenagers became, not the four-ounce hamburger but our old friend the Big Mac). These are all good reasons. Lack of exercise in childhood, with fewer children walking to school, often results in obese teenagers. But why do people stay obese? Why don't they lose weight when they realize how dangerous it can be to carry too much fat around? According to Landsburg, it is because they have lost the incentive to lose weight. And incentives, as we know, are the key to economic behaviour. He writes:

> *Here's one plausible story: The nineties saw the advent of drugs like Pravachol and Lipitor that can dramatically cut your cholesterol and increase your life expectancy. With medical advances like that, who needs to be thin? Of course obesity is still bad for you – but it's not as bad for you as it used to be. The price of obesity (measured in health risks) is down, so rational consumers will choose more of it. With the success of the human genome project, even greater advances are just over the horizon, making obesity an even greater bargain. Today's expanding waistlines might reflect nothing more than a rational expectation of future progress against heart disease.*

Landsburg also offers, perhaps tongue in cheek, an explanation of why low-fat foods contribute to obesity.

Suppose a scoop of ice cream a night would add 10 pounds to your weight, and you've decided that's not worth it, so you don't eat ice cream. Now along comes a low-fat ice cream that allows you to eat two scoops a night and add 10 pounds to your weight. That's a better deal, and a perfectly rational being might well opt for it. So when low-fat foods come along, some people sensibly decide to become fatter.

Economists, you see, have an explanation for everything. Why do tall people tend to be more successful in life? The usual explanation is that employers favour them, particularly in leadership positions. There is, however, little evidence of that. And if there was evidence of such discrimination, short people could legitimately cry foul. The key, according to researchers at Pennsylvania State University is that what matters is not height in adulthood but height during adolescence. Tall adolescents are usually picked for school sports teams, are chosen as prefects and, in the case of boys at least, often fare better with the opposite sex. It is during adolescence that, thanks to their height, the tall acquire both confidence and leadership qualities. This explains, incidentally, why some short people have risen to the top. Very often they will have been tall for their age during adolescence and then stopped growing. Does it work as a general rule? Ask around.

Work or leisure?
Finally in this section, let me come to a question of incentives that causes much debate among economists. When somebody

wins a large sum on the football pools, the lottery or *Who Wants to Be a Millionaire?* the question usually asked is: will your winnings mean that you will give up work? There is another question, to which I shall return later in the book, which is: will this money make you happy? In response to the work question, the answer is either the heart-warming but probably unrealistic: 'I won't let it change my life,' or the more usual: 'You bet your life I'm giving up work.'

Very few of us win large sums of money, although the prospect of doing so gives us an incentive to play the lottery or do the pools, however long the odds. But many of us are faced with smaller versions of this kind of decision. Suppose, at a time of negligible inflation, you receive a 25 per cent pay rise. The choice is between being better off financially or, instead, working four days a week instead of five and enjoying the same standard of living as before. A manager could, in other words, reward his best staff by paying them more, only to find that he then sees less of them.

This is known as the 'work–leisure trade-off' and it is quite interesting and important. By leisure, by the way, we do not mean just going to the cinema or lounging around the pool. It also includes those hours you spend sleeping, washing up or cleaning out the drains, in other words all non-work hours. If you spent all the time working, not only would you be very tired, but there would be no time to spend the money you had earned. That is one end of the spectrum in terms of the work–leisure trade-off. If you did not work at all but spent all your time on the beach, you would have no money to eat. That is the other end of the spectrum. For most people there will be a trade-off between work and leisure somewhere in the middle. To go back to the earlier discussion of why people spend in the way they do, people will be 'indifferent' between a certain amount of time spent in work, say forty hours a week, and a certain amount of leisure, the rest of the week. When wages rise people are indeed better off, and could work fewer hours. On the other hand, leisure has become relatively more expensive – think how much you could be earning while you are relaxing – creating an incentive to work longer hours. The balance between these two effects, the income and substitution effects, will determine whether higher wages result in longer or shorter hours.

On the face of it, the long-run evidence suggests that higher wages do result in fewer hours worked. I described in the last chapter how incomes have risen in real terms – they have outstripped inflation – but alongside this we have also seen a decline in hours worked. In the past fifty years or so, a typical manual worker's week has dropped from forty-eight hours to forty or fewer, with a corresponding reduction in the standard white-collar week. Prosperity brought with it a demand for greater leisure – the income effect dominated the substitution effect. To remind you how this works, the rise in income has, in effect, made it possible to buy more leisure time, and this is what most people have chosen to do. This is despite the fact that leisure time has become more expensive in terms of what the worker could have earned by, say, working Saturday mornings.

Interestingly, many would testify that this process came to an end in the 1990s, with many managerial and white-collar staff being required to work far longer than their statutory hours of employment, and to take work home. More people took second jobs, notably in America and Britain. There are also big variations in working hours, even among industrial countries. Americans work more than 1,900 hours a year, compared with fewer than 1,600 in Germany and about 1,700 in Britain. The differences are accounted for by variations in both weekly hours and holiday entitlements.

Work and tax

All this is rather important, particularly when it comes to economic policy. In the 1980s, when Margaret Thatcher was in office in Britain and Ronald Reagan was in the White House, there was great stress on the role of incentives and on how they could be sharpened by means of income tax cuts. The argument was that if you allowed people to keep more of their earnings – in effect boosting their wages – they would work harder. If you hit them with punitive rates of tax, on the other hand, they would work less hard. Embarrassingly for the British government, a piece of research commissioned by the Treasury and carried out by Professor Chuck Brown of Stirling University found that the opposite was true. When taxes were cut, it either made no difference to people or they worked fewer hours. But when taxes went up, they were obliged to work harder to maintain their level of (post-tax) income. A furious debate ensued, after which there was no clear winner. Most people, it turned out, were in no real position to alter their hours of work, these being fixed by the firm they worked for. The more difficult question of whether lower taxes meant they worked harder during their allotted time, in other words raised their productivity, is still not conclusively settled.

I shall return to tax later. One area where tax changes do appear to have had a clear effect on people's appetite for work is in the case of women. In Britain married couples used to be taxed jointly. A woman getting a part-time job would be taxed at her husband's highest marginal tax rate, which in the 1970s in Britain could be as high as 83 per cent and for most of the 1980s was, for higher-rate taxpayers, 60 per cent. In such circumstances many couples decided it was not worth the wife working. Independent taxation, the separate taxation of husbands and wives, introduced in the late 1980s by Nigel Lawson, one of Thatcher's three Chancellors, changed all this. Women had their own tax-free allowance and paid tax at a rate that reflected their earnings, not those of their husbands. This made a big contribution to one of the features of Britain's job market in the latter part of the twentieth century – a huge increase in the number of women working.

**
*

We have come a long way and we are not even through the main course yet. I know the feeling, however, when you are halfway through a prestige dinner with the speeches still to come, and you are wondering uncomfortably whether you can make it until the end. I also hate excessively long chapters. It is time for a quick comfort break, and then to welcome a very special guest.

4

Adam –
but no apple

In many ways our first celebrity guest is a brave choice. While
few economists would quarrel with the choice of Adam Smith
(1723–90) as the father of modern economics, many might hesitate before inviting him along as a speaker. This eighteenth century Scot was almost a parody of the absent-minded professor.
Anecdotes that have been passed down through the years tell of
him putting bread and butter into a teapot, pouring hot water on
it, and then wondering why the tea tasted so foul. Or of him
being so engaged in a philosophical discourse while walking
along that he stumbled into a tanning pit. Born in Kirkcaldy on
the Firth of Forth a few months after the death of his father, the
town's customs controller (in the days when the post was
grander than now), Smith never married, although he refers

approvingly in print to the beauty of 'potato-fed Irish prostitutes' in London. He was no oil painting, as he himself admitted. While in later life women courted his mind, they had to overcome his big teeth and bulging eyes. One female French novelist declared him to be 'ugly as the devil'. His private passions have to be a source of speculation because he ordered all his papers to be destroyed on his death.

Smith, like many great thinkers, was not, it seems, a great speaker. Burdened with a harsh voice and an occasional stutter, he was also an unforgiving lecturer. Having spent a miserable few years in Oxford as a student, he chose his native Scotland to pursue his academic career. His lectures in Glasgow used to start at 7.30 in the morning, begin hesitantly, and then last for hours, with Smith addressing the ceiling rather than the students. He was sometimes seen carrying on such debates with himself out loud, on street corners. Absent-minded he may have been but he was also hugely influential. Two centuries after his death his ideas returned to prominence across the world but, in particular, with the election of Ronald Reagan in America and Margaret Thatcher in Britain. Thatcher was said to carry a copy of Smith's *The Wealth of Nations* in her legendary and capacious handbag. The Adam Smith Institute in London (on whose website those with stamina can read the 900-page work) came to the fore as an advocate of privatization and pro-market policies. The collapse of communism and the triumph of capitalism at the end of the 1980s could be seen as a victory for Smith over Karl Marx.

Timing is everything

As far as economists were concerned, Smith had never gone away. It may seem like a conceit to think that economics began in 1776 with the publication of his great work which, to give it its full title, was *An Inquiry into the Nature and Causes of the Wealth of Nations* (in his lifetime it was outsold by his other main work, *The Theory of Moral Sentiments*). There was economics before Smith, now known as pre-Adamite economics. Ancient civilizations had their economic thinkers, as did the Renaissance. Like all great thinkers Smith has been accused of lifting some of his best ideas from his predecessors and near contemporaries. Certainly he was fortunate in some respects. He was offered and accepted a lucrative sinecure from Charles Townshend, a fan of *The Theory of Moral Sentiments* and one-time Chancellor of the Exchequer, who invited him to become tutor to his teenage stepson, the Duke of Buccleuch. On taking up this role, in which he began the twelve-year period of the writing of *The Wealth of Nations*, Smith travelled widely with his pupil, and was able to tap into economic thinking elsewhere in Europe. French economists such as François Quesnay were influential. He also spent time with Voltaire.

The important thing about *The Wealth of Nations*, however, hugely ambitious as it was in scope and size, is that it presented the first synthesis of economics in its entirety. It explained why nations should trade with each other and benefit from doing so (opposing the view of the earlier mercantilists who had favoured trade restrictions in the belief that protectionism preserved economic advantage for some countries). It provided an explanation and a justification for the minimum interference by government in free markets within countries. It told governments how they should go about the process of raising taxes. It explained how the industrial revolution then in progress would raise prosperity, most notably as we shall see with his famous example of the pin factory.

That, perhaps, helps explain Smith's influence more than anything. He came at a turning point in economic history. Published in the year of American independence and the beginning of a new world order, *The Wealth of Nations* also coincided with the start of a process in which industrialization was to provide unprecedented growth in wealth. This, a step-change compared with the economic stagnation of the agricultural age, was also to raise questions about how that wealth should be distributed among the population. Smith, a product of the Enlightenment, provided a template for economic thinking through and beyond the industrial revolution that utterly changed previous notions about the way societies worked.

But what, out of the multi-volume *Wealth of Nations*, should we take as important? Is it Smith's rules, or canons, of taxation, centred on ability to pay? Is it his theory of value? Is it his belief that governments should concentrate on certain basic functions, because most public services are 'unproductive', and that public works such as roads or bridges should be paid for by tolls or fees, not out of general taxation? Important though these are to students of the history of economic thought and in some cases to policymakers today, and while it is the done thing at this point to recommend that people read the full work themselves (few do), there are three things we should carry with us from Smith.

The division of labour

Smith was writing at a time when there were very few factories in Britain. Those that did exist were mainly powered by water. The industrial revolution had barely begun. Yet he promised to demonstrate how economic changes could occur that would bring 'universal opulence which extends itself to the lowest ranks of the people'. First among these was the division of labour. The pin factory, mentioned above, demonstrates very simply how this operates. Suppose, Smith said, a pin factory employed ten people, each engaged in the entire process of making a pin. The factory would certainly produce pins, perhaps a few hundred a day, but it would not do so very effectively. Now look at the way it actually worked in his day: 'One man draws out the wire, another straightens it, a third cuts it, a fourth points it, a fifth grinds it at the top for receiving a head; to make the head requires two or three distinct operations; to put it on is a peculiar business, to whiten the pins is another; it is even a trade by itself to put them into the paper.'

And so on. Specialization made each man much more effect-ive. Even in what was essentially a manual process, without the machinery that was to shape industrialization, huge productivity gains could be achieved. The division of labour, in other words, raised the level of output per worker. Smith's factory produced not a few hundred but tens of thousands of pins each day. It is interesting to think that it took until 1912, when Henry Ford applied his mass production methods to the building of the

Model T at his Highland Park assembly plant in America, methods that meant the time it took to build a car was cut to just ninety-three minutes, for the full flowering of this particular division of labour to occur.

There was more to Smith's division of labour, however, than a management consultant's approach to factory organization. If we think about the pin factory, the key to raising the productivity of the workers and therefore their prosperity and that of the owners was specialization. But there was no reason, as Smith explained, to think of the possibilities of specialization as being limited to those within a single workplace.

What determines why some people do certain jobs and others do others? In general, people find something they are suited to and good at. What is best for me to do, to try to fix a problem with the plumbing in my house in my inexpert and laborious way? Or to write an article (or probably, given the prices London plumbers charge, two or three articles) to earn the money to pay for the services of a professional? The answer, to me at least, is fairly clear, as I hope it would be to the plumber if somebody asked him to pen an economics piece. The point is that it is much more efficient if each of us concentrates on what we are good at and trade those services. We buy pork chops from the butcher rather than attempt to kill the pig for ourselves.

Extending this division of labour a little further up the scale, it becomes clearly beneficial if there is specialization by firms. A modern car is made up of many hundreds of components manufactured by different firms. Such specialization enables the cost of the car to be much lower than if a single firm attempted to make every part. In the 1980s there was a revolution in British industry when manufacturing firms contracted out to independent suppliers many tasks, from cleaning and maintenance to distribution. They were following Adam Smith.

The process does not have to end within countries. The argument in favour of foreign trade, indeed of free trade, is essentially a division of labour argument. With the right investment in hothouses and specialist equipment, Britain could in theory provide for all her wine needs and never import a drop from abroad. It makes more sense, however, to buy it from countries with the climate and expertise to do it better and more cheaply. The basis of trade is that countries specialize in the things they are best at. The gains from trade result from this specialization. This is why action to restrict trade usually impoverishes us all. What happens if a country is no good at anything? I'll come back to that later.

The invisible hand

The part of *The Wealth of Nations* that every schoolchild knows – or if not they should – gives us Smith's most famous idea. He wrote: 'It is not from the benevolence of the butcher, the brewer, or the baker, that we expect our dinner, but from their regard to their own interest. We address ourselves not to their humanity but their self love.'

To understand it fully, it is necessary to tie it to another, related section which, in slightly edited form, reads: 'Every individual who employs capital and labours neither intends to promote the public interest nor knows how much he is promoting it … he is led by an invisible hand which was no part of his intention. By pursuing his own interest he frequently promotes that of society.'

What was this invisible hand? Because of its later importance, you might think there are references to it dotted throughout the pages of *The Wealth of Nations*. In fact the above is the only one. Some writers have speculated that it could have had religious connotations; others that Smith unconsciously lifted it from Shakespeare's *Macbeth*, where there is a reference to the 'bloody and invisible hand'.

There is no need to get too fancy about this, however. What Smith was sketching out was the market mechanism, the laws of supply and demand we have already touched on, although it was left to later economists to fill in the details. This was no paean of praise to businessmen. Whenever they met 'the conversation ends in a conspiracy against the public, or in some contrivance to raise prices'. The point was that the market did not let them get away with it, or at least not for long. Customers would abandon profiteers in favour of competitors offering lower prices. Attempts by groups of firms to fix prices by agreement – forming a cartel – would fail as long as it was possible for new firms to enter the market and undercut them. The invisible hand is the market, and through its operation the best possible, or optimum, outcome is achieved. Of course in any economy there will be lots of different markets, not only for all the various products and services, but also, for example, for labour. One of the great debates sparked off by Smith was, in fact, over labour. What was to stop workers being permanently exploited in this new industrial revolution, of being paid no more than necessary for the very basics of existence? Smith pointed out not only that competition for workers among employers would make this unlikely but also that the process of industrialization and of the development of mass market products would require that workers – as the new consumers – be paid above the subsistence level, and increasingly so. He was right. The market did not put an end to worker exploitation but the industrial revolution marked the start of the rise of modern mass prosperity. As we shall see, Karl Marx had rather different views on this.

Liberty

It is hard to overstate the importance of Smith's contribution to economics. As its founding father he provided a template for it and an underlying philosophy that endures to this day – that economic freedom provides the best of all possible worlds, through the operation of the invisible hand. Attempts to interfere with that freedom by introducing restrictions or allowing monopolies to operate will make us all poorer than we need be. Governments, even if they mean well, will usually end up making things worse. This did not mean there should be no government at all – Smith favoured strong and clear laws, properly policed – but it did mean limiting its role. Smith would have had no truck with government being directly involved in the production process by owning firms.

When, advocated by the likes of Margaret Thatcher, Smith came back into vogue, it was easy to see why. The market, it seemed, had taken a back seat. The UK had in the thirty or so years since the Second World War become a heavily controlled economy and one in which the state played an increasingly dominant role. Monopoly power had been allowed to develop while, on the other side, unions operated a range of restrictive practices. The policies followed by the Thatcher governments, which involved the removal of controls, denationalization (or as it came to be known, privatization), and the ending of restrictive practices by both unions and employers added up to a classic recipe for restoring markets, for giving the invisible hand a chance to operate. Adam Smith would have been proud of her.

5

Main course (2)

Welcome back. Before we broke we had made a lot of progress in trying to explain how, as individuals, we behave as economic animals, even when we are not aware of it. All very interesting, you might say (at least I hope you do), but how does this fit into the big picture? When people talk about 'the economy', what do they mean? This is a good time to start thinking big, to go from the micro to the macro.

So what is an economy?

This is one of those questions, a bit like 'What is life, Daddy?', you hope your children will not ask you. The best way of answering it, given that this is probably not the time for another food analogy, is by thinking of a football match. At one level, a football match is a game between two teams of eleven men lasting ninety minutes, the object of which is to kick a round object into your opponents' goal more times than they do into yours. Everybody knows, however, there is more to it than that. A football match is about the contributions of individual players, and of the referee and crowd, about the goals, the goalmouth incidents, the fouls, the mistakes. Put like that, a football match consists of many thousands of actions that combine to make a whole. How do you explain that to somebody who was not there? They can read a match report in the newspaper. If they are real enthusiasts, though, they will examine the statistics – goals scored, shots on goal, red and yellow cards, the percentage of time each team had possession of the ball, and so on. The statistics can never be a perfect substitute for being there but they are the next best thing. So it is with the economy. At its most basic the British economy is what a nation of roughly 60 million people spend, earn and produce. At its most complicated it is the millions upon millions of decisions taken by individuals, either for themselves or on behalf of companies. Magnificent though this would be to observe, it would also be impossible. As with football, therefore, it is necessary to boil all these actions down to manageable statistics. For economists, as we shall see later, it is also necessary to develop models of the economy. These simplified or stylized versions of the real thing are similar in concept to architects' models of buildings. An architect's model does not try to capture every detail of the actual building – very few have running water or working miniature coffee machines – but they give a good idea of what the full-sized building will look like. Economic models try for something similar. Disappointingly, however, when economists say they are building a model of the economy, this does not mean they are getting out the hard-board, sticky-backed plastic and papier-mâché. Models of the economy are usually linked sets of mathematical equations that churn away in the recesses of computers. One of the exceptions, still in existence at the Science Museum in London, was built at the London School of Economics.

In the late 1940s A. W. 'Bill' Phillips was a New Zealander in his early thirties who had emerged from a Japanese prisoner-of-war-camp (Laurens van der Post, Prince Charles's mentor, was a fellow prisoner). Phillips had suffered near starvation, as was obvi-ous to fellow students when he came to study at the LSE. He also had difficulty understanding what he was being taught and in par-ticular the flow of money around the economy. So, using Perspex tubes, levers, pulleys and windscreen-wiper motors scavenged from a wartime plane, he built a model of it. It was and is a device of extraordinary complexity. Not only was it a fully working hydraulic model showing money (water) flowing around the system but it also provided a primitive printout, as a pen attached to the machine plotted the results. When Phillips demonstrated the machine to a sceptical LSE audience in 1949 by pouring in red liquid at the top to demonstrate the effects of adding cash to the economy, there was general acclaim. The model, conceived in an age when computers were still the stuff of science fiction to most people, could simulate the effects of, say, cutting taxes or boost-ing government spending. *Punch*, the humorous magazine, said a Phillips machine should be installed in every town hall in Britain. 'The machine is taller than the man in the street and wider and heavier and much, much cleverer,' it said. 'Using coloured water (a convenience denied the man in the street) it reacts obediently to every morsel of economic information communicated to it, and records, with its mechanical pens on its calibrated charts, the subtle impact of a slump in the second-hand ship market, the slightest hint of a boom in soap, emery wheels or white fish.' Phillips did not make one of his machines for every town hall but he did make fourteen of them. The Ford Motor Company bought one, and so did Harvard. Phillips went on to become an influential economist. Computers, initially bigger and more unwieldy than his machine, took over the job of running models of the economy – which was a pity.

Anyway, let me return to the question of trying to pin the economy down a little more closely.

Adding it all up

Until about 100 years ago, economists knew, or thought they knew, what the economy was but they had no means of measuring it. When William Gladstone was Chancellor of the Exchequer in the nineteenth century he had no difficulty in finding things to talk about. Most modern Chancellors manage to get through their annual Budget speeches in about an hour. Gladstone made one last more than four hours, and this was without the benefit of the kind of macroeconomic statistics regarded as essential today. Britain's Central Statistical Office, now called the Office for National Statistics, was not set up until 1941, because at the time it was recognized that there was an urgent need for accurate and timely statistics on production, particularly of munitions, and of the supply–demand situation for scarce food. During the war Britain effectively became a command economy, with 70 per cent of it government controlled but the statistical tradition continued and was extended in peacetime. Nowadays, within a couple of months, we know to one decimal place how much the economy grew in the most recent quarter. The figures, like most economic statistics, are subject to revision but they are still testimony to how far the art of measurement has advanced.

Most people, understandably, do not worry overmuch about whether the economy grew by 0.2 or 0.8 per cent in the latest quarter, leaving such matters to those whose job it is to pore over the statistics. It does matter, of course. The economy's long-run growth rate is about 0.6 per cent a quarter, or about 2.5 per cent a year. If growth stayed at this rate, year-in year-out, you would expect unemployment to remain steady. Why? Because each year we become more productive, increasing our output by 2 per cent or so compared with the previous year. A lot of people do not believe this and think of themselves as being about as productive as they have always been. Think, though, of the way technology has replaced, for example, so many basic clerking functions in offices. If the economy did not grow at all or did so only slowly, then rising productivity would mean fewer workers were needed, hence rising unemployment. If it grows roughly in line with productivity, unemployment remains stable. Higher growth rates should mean falling unemployment, and vice versa. If the economy shrinks even for a quarter ('negative growth' is the clumsy term most economists use for this), the worry would be recession. If it grew by 1.5 per cent in that quarter, the worry would be the opposite one of 'overheating'. All this will become clearer a little later.

The most useful thing about macroeconomic data, and in particular the national accounts, is not the precise information it gives us about any single quarter or year. It is, rather, that it gives us an invaluable framework for thinking about how the economy is constructed. If it were possible to observe the economy from above, it would consist of many millions of transactions by people spending, producing and earning. That is exactly what gross domestic product (GDP), the main measure of the size of the economy and of changes in that size – economic growth – seeks to measure. GDP is the sum of everything produced in the economy, hence gross domestic *product*. To avoid double counting, however, it is necessary to subtract at each stage the value of the inputs that have gone into producing a product. The chef in our expensive restaurant assembles and cooks the meal. He could not do it, however, without the vegetables supplied from the market that morning, the meat from the butcher or the gas or electricity supplied by the power company. His output, for the purposes of measuring GDP, is the value added to these various inputs. The same applies from the very largest company, making billions each year, to the smallest sole trader. The principle is exactly the same as value added tax, VAT. Some people, indeed, prefer to talk, not of GDP, but of 'gross value-added'.

Hang on though, where do earning and spending fit in? Do they fit in? The answer is that they do. GDP is often known as national income. The two are not precisely the same but broadly similar. GDP, as well as being the sum of everything produced in the economy, or at least the value added at each stage of production, is also the sum of incomes earned. It is easy to see why this should be. The income of our chef, assuming he is also the owner of the restaurant, is the amount we have paid him for the meal less the wages of his staff, the income earned by his suppliers and, say, the rent for the premises (the landlord's income), which he has been obliged to pay. The value of the income earned by the various players equals the value of production.

You may ask at this point how this relates to your own circumstances. Suppose you are a salaried employee for a profitable firm. Your income, plainly, goes to make up GDP. But what about the profit the company makes? What about the tax you pay? Profit is easy enough. That is either reinvested, in which case it generates income for the suppliers of capital equipment. Or it is distributed to shareholders in the form of dividends, which means income for them. Tax is a little trickier. On the face of it, it simply represents the income of government. In practice, the way to think about tax is in terms of the income it generates as the government converts tax into public spending, thus providing income for doctors, nurses, teachers and civil servants, as well as payments to state pensioners and people on welfare benefits. These last are known as 'transfer payments' because they are simply transfer money between taxpayers and beneficiaries.

It really does all add up. GDP is not only the value of everything produced (the value added) in the economy, but also the sum of incomes received. It is also, and I have left what I regard as the most useful until last, the sum of spending.

The most useful equation in economics

So how does spending fit in? Again, the important thing to avoid in measuring the economy is double counting. What we are therefore concerned with is 'final' demand. When you or I buy a car, we have probably read the brochure beforehand detailing all the features and accessories it comes equipped with. What we are concerned with, however, is the entire product. Few people would buy a car and then remove the radio to sell it, or the spare wheel. Similarly, the purchase of all these components by the manufacturer does not feature in GDP. Such purchases are known as 'intermediate demand'. The car could not be made without them but they are subsumed in final demand.

Does that mean that spending by consumers is all that matters? After all, if we are talking about final demand, it would seem natural that most of that comes from you and me when we shop. Consumer spending, or household consumption as it is now known by the official statisticians in Britain, does indeed account for the lion's share of GDP, but not all of it. In the year 2000, for example, UK consumer spending totalled £595 billion (that's £595,000 million). That in itself is quite an interesting figure, being the equivalent of £10,000 for every man, woman and child in the country. GDP, however, was higher than this, at £943 billion. So consumer spending accounted for most of it, 63 per cent, a typical figure. I have used the UK as an example but this is typical of most advanced economies. Consumers drive our economies. After the 11 September 2001 terrorist attacks on America the key question for economists was whether consumers would lose their nerve. Incidentally, you often hear economists and pundits gravely opining that whether the economy slows or not depends on the consumer. I have done it myself. As you can see, there is nothing terribly profound about this. As a matter of simple arithmetic it mainly does depend on the consumer and the rate of growth of consumer spending depends mainly on the rate of growth of income (this is known as the 'consumption function'). But where does the rest of the spending that makes up GDP come from?

The next most important category, in Britain at least, is spending by government. Again, this is quite typical. The national accounts showed that for the year 2000 the government spent £175 billion. This is a big number but it is also a little puzzling. As a proportion of GDP it is a little under 19 per cent but, as many people will know, both public expenditure and tax in Britain are usually thought of as being roughly 40 per cent of GDP. If spending were really only 19 per cent of GDP, taxes could be much lower. What has happened to the missing 20 per cent or so? The answer, mainly, is that for GDP purposes it is necessary to exclude transfer payments, such as state pensions and benefits, which account for a lot of government spending but which, in economic terms, is money the government hands over to other people to spend. This is not true, by the way, of the salaries of public sector workers such as teachers or nurses. When the government pays them, it is buying the services of these professionals, just as your purchase of the services of a plumber counts as part of consumer spending.

The other missing bit of government spending comes in our next GDP category, investment. When a business buys a computer, that is investment. When a household does so, it is consumer spending. Most investment in Britain is done by the private sector, on plant, machinery, vehicles and so on. But government, often now in partnership with the private sector, also carries out investment. New hospitals, roads, government computers, for instance, count as part of investment, or 'gross fixed capital formation', as statisticians usually describe it. Investment in productive capacity, as every businessman knows, is vital for long-run economic growth. For many years it was thought that Japan's economic success was due to high levels of investment, averaging 30 per cent of GDP. More recently, Japan's economic problems, together with those in other Asian economies, have raised the question about whether, as far as investment is concerned, it is possible to have too much of a good thing. In Britain in the year 2000 investment totalled £165 billion, or just over 17 per cent of GDP.

Adding up spending by consumers, spending by government and investment gives us, for the year 2000, 63 plus 19 plus 17 per cent, or 99 per cent in total. Give or take the 1 per cent for rounding, it appears we have got to GDP. Well, we would have, but only if we lived in a 'closed' economy with no overseas trade. What we are measuring, albeit via different categories of spending, is gross domestic *product*, in other words the value of spending on goods and services produced in Britain. That Japanese DVD player or German car included in consumer spending – quite a lot of them actually – should not be part of Britain's GDP (although the proportion of the selling price that reflects distribution costs within Britain and the retailer's profit should be). At the same time, there are plenty of products and services produced in Britain but consumed in other countries. GDP therefore also has to reflect exports and imports. Exports are goods and services made here but consumed elsewhere. Imports are made elsewhere but consumed here.

In 2000 exports totalled £265 billion, equivalent to 28 per cent of GDP. We add this £265 billion to the totals for consumer spending, government outlays and investment. Imports, on the other hand, were £281 billion, 30 per cent of GDP. We take this away from our GDP total. The fact that both exports and imports were roughly 30 per cent of GDP shows that Britain is an open economy, as it has been for centuries. Both America and Japan, the world's two biggest economies at the time of writing (Britain has sneaked back up to fourth place), have much smaller export–import shares. The fact that imports exceeded exports shows that Britain was running a trade deficit.

This book is intended to be an equation-free zone, but GDP $= C + G + I + X - M$ is a way of setting down simply what has been spelt out above. Strictly speaking it is not an equation at all but an 'identity'. C is consumer spending, G government spending, I investment, X exports and M imports. Sometimes you will see instead of GDP the letter Y (for reasons that have never been entirely clear to me), for national income, but the meaning is the same.

Why is this so useful? First, it provides a simple way to understand explanation of the various types of spending that drive the economy. Second, anybody trying to forecast what will happen to the economy will first need to predict what is likely to happen to these expenditure components of GDP. All the main models of the economy are based around this simple identity. It also provides, with the accompanying statistical information, a rough idea of the orders of magnitude involved. A 1 per cent rise in consumer spending, for example, increases GDP by about 0.6 per cent, but it would take an increase in investment of more than 3 per cent, or a rise in exports of over 2 per cent, to produce the same effect.

Does it really add up?

Sharp-eyed readers who have been working out GDP for themselves will have noticed that they come up with an answer £20 billion or so short of the £943 billion we are looking for. There are two reasons for this. One is that the statisticians in Britain separate out from other consumer spending the small amount of spending by non-profit institutions – charities and not-for-profit companies – on behalf of households. The other is that some of what is produced in any given year is not sold but goes into stocks, or inventories. Inventories can be important in determining quarter-on-quarter or year-on-year movements in GDP. At the onset of recession, for example, there is often an unplanned build-up in stocks of unsold goods. But the big picture for GDP is provided by our five other components: C, G, I, X and M.

There is one other little complication. Much of what we spend our money on is subject to tax. Taxes such as VAT and excise duties are known as 'indirect' taxation whereas taxes on income, such as most obviously income tax and also National Insurance, are known as 'direct' taxation. Included in the total

for consumer spending, for example, will therefore be a significant indirect tax element. Many goods, roughly half, are subject
to VAT at 17.5 per cent. In theory the government could temporarily boost GDP simply by increasing VAT, although the
subsequent effect of that should be to make us spend less.
Because of this tax complication, economists usually distinguish
between GDP at 'market prices' – the prices that are actually
paid – and GDP at 'factor cost', which is those same prices
excluding the tax element. The difference between the two
measures is simply the amount of indirect taxation, in other
words GDP at market prices less indirect taxes equals GDP at
factor cost. Again, there is no need to worry about this distinction. The two measures will not show much variation when it
comes to measuring economic growth except when there are
big changes in indirect taxation such as in 1979, when Margaret
Thatcher's Conservative government increased VAT to 15 per
cent, from the old rates of 8 and 12.5 per cent, or in 1991, when
the Conservatives raised VAT again, from 15 to 17.5 per cent.
The market price/factor cost difference is worth keeping by
you, however, if only for one-upmanship purposes, invaluable
in economics.

Does housework have any value?

All the above, I hope, will have seemed entirely logical. There
is, however, a long-running debate in economics about whether
GDP and closely related measures are comprehensive enough.
The problem arises because plenty of activity goes unmeasured
in the economy. This is not just the kind of activity that people

deliberately keep away from the taxman, the so-called black economy – thought to be worth between 5 and 15 per cent of GDP in most countries – but also much more mundane things. If two of us go to the local park and exhaust ourselves playing tennis for a couple of hours, then, apart from the small amount we have paid to hire the court and perhaps buy a couple of new balls, the effect on GDP is negligible. If, on the other hand, two professionals slog it out for a considerable amount of prize money on the Centre Court at Wimbledon, there is quite a sizeable GDP effect. Many would say this is as it should be. Plenty of people are prepared to pay good money to watch the professionals but you could not give away tickets to witness my efforts.

Much more difficult questions arise in respect of housework. Mr Jones, a gentleman of some means, employs a housekeeper, Miss Williams. She is courteous and efficient and he pays her a good wage. She is also very pretty. Soon the inevitable happens and love blossoms over the feather duster. They marry and, while she carries on much as before with the housework, he stops paying her a wage. After all, in marriage what is his is hers. The effect, however, is to reduce GDP. Before the marriage part of his spending was on her housekeeping services. And, while she was paid out of his income, her earnings counted separately for GDP purposes. These effects, which are identical, reduce the expenditure and income measures of GDP respectively, while the value of her output is also apparently lost to the national economy.

Can this be right? Plenty of people think not. For almost as long as there have been national accounts, there have been people arguing for the inclusion of non-paid housework, as well as the many other unpaid but useful activities without which the economy would grind to a halt. Work on a so-called 'genuine progress index' in the province of Nova Scotia, Canada, found that people put in 941 million hours a year on domestic chores and primary childcare, 1,230 hours per adult. This was 25 per cent more than the 707 million hours a year of paid work in Nova Scotia. When the researchers valued this unpaid work at the prevailing pay rates for domestic work and childcare they found it added up to just over half of measured GDP. Including this unpaid work, in other words, would push up the level of GDP by half as much again.

As they put it:

Work performed in households is more essential to basic survival and quality of life than much of the work done in offices, factories and stores, and is a fundamental precondition for a healthy market sector. If children are not reared with attention and care, and if household members are not provided with nutritious sustenance, workplace productivity will decline and social costs will rise. Physical maintenance of the housing stock, including cleaning and repairs, is also essential economic activity. Yet this huge unpaid contribution registers nowhere in our standard economic accounts. When we pay for childcare and house cleaning, and when we eat out, this adds to GDP and counts as economic growth and 'progress'. When we cook our own meals, clean our own house and look after our own children it has no value in our measures of progress.

It is a persuasive argument, and it has its echoes in the currently fashionable debate about the 'work–life balance', that the way we have come to work and live overstates the economic and social value of time spent at the office (it usually is the office) or factory. Unfortunately, there would be very real problems in trying to include unpaid activity in the national accounts. GDP, as we have seen, is made up of a huge number of recorded transactions. What happens when there is no recorded transaction? Do we assume that a husband will pay his wife the going market rate for doing the housework (or, if he is a house-husband, vice versa)? If so, why should the couple not just employ somebody to do the job? If the value the husband or wife puts on the housework is less than the market rate, how much less is it? We really do not know and it would be very difficult to find out. Official statisticians have enough trouble trying to monitor recorded transactions. GDP may be an incomplete measure of the amount of activity in the economy but for the moment it is the best we have. Despite these problems, the UK's Office for National Statistics had a go in 2002 at estimating the value of unpaid work in the home, including food preparation, washing, ironing, transporting children around, and so on. Its estimate was £700 billion. While stressing that its estimate should be treated with caution, it noted that the value of this so-called household production was equivalent to 77 per cent of adjusted GDP, more than in Canada.

Shoppers and savers
As far as individuals are concerned, they have so far been seen

in action, at both microeconomic and macroeconomic levels, as workers helping in the production process, as earners and, of course, as spenders, quite big spenders at that. What has not yet been touched on is the role of individuals as savers. We know that this is important. Look at the personal finance pages of any newspaper, or the size of a financial services industry supported largely by personal saving. Over the long term households in Britain save an average of 10 per cent of disposable income (take-home pay), although this proportion, known as the 'saving ratio', has been lower in recent years. Saving, encouraged by successive British governments via tax relief on, for example, personal equity plans (Peps), tax-exempt special savings accounts (Tessas) and individual savings accounts (Isas), is generally regarded as a good thing. Most governments provide some form of incentive to save. If there has been a shift in recent years it has been away from the self-interested encouragement by governments of saving in products such as Premium Bonds and National Savings certificates, which are a way of packaging and thus funding government debt. Most obviously in wartime but also at other times, people have been persuaded to help the government to fund its debt by buying bonds, war loans or other products. These days, governments are keen to encourage saving not only for its own sake but also to provide the resources for productive investment. In a closed economy with no government, the only source of funds for investment, in fact, would be from the amount people put aside for saving. Things are rather more complicated in an open economy with no capital controls (which means that funds can and do flow in and out of the country), but the general point still stands.

Countries with very low saving ratios are generally either not investing enough or they are excessively dependent on funds flowing in from overseas. At the tail end of the long US economic boom of the 1990s, when the saving ratio dropped to zero alongside still strong investment, many economists expressed concern that this was not a sustainable situation. In the event investment fell sharply when the economy slowed. Japan, again, long provided the example to the rest of the industrialized world, with saving as well as investment equivalent to about 30 per cent of GDP. Latterly though, the Japanese economy could have done with consumers spending more and saving rather less. Japan, in fact, may be a living example of what is known as 'the paradox of thrift'. The paradox is that, while a high level of saving is beneficial in the long term, providing the funds for investment and therefore for strengthening the economy's ability to grow, in the short term more saving (and therefore less spending) means a lower rate of economic growth, which may itself discourage firms from investing.

What makes people save?

Surely it cannot be patriotic duty that makes people save, or a need to ensure there are sufficient funds for productive investment to take place. It is not hard to find reasons for saving – putting money away in case of unforeseen emergencies, such as loss of income, for the 'rainy day' of legend, for school or university fees, or for retirement. Milton Friedman, most famous as the intellectual parent of the monetarism of the 1970s and 1980s, gave us the permanent income hypothesis. This advanced the argument that people have a firm idea of what their permanent or long-run income is, and how much they want to spend out of that income to maintain a certain standard of living. If in one year they receive a large bonus, they are too canny to regard that as part of their permanent income, and so will save a significant proportion of it by buying financial assets. If in another year their pay is cut because times are tough, they may also treat that as temporary, maintaining their spending by drawing down savings. Saving varies according to what people actually earn in relation to their permanent income.

If this sounds a bit too good to be true, Franco Modigliani and Albert Ando offered their life-cycle hypothesis of saving behaviour. At its simplest this is just a story about pensions. People build up savings during periods when they are earning most and run them down when their earnings stop, during retirement. We are spenders rather than savers in childhood, accumulate savings during middle age (or give some of it to our own children to spend) and run down savings in old age, probably leaving some spare at the end to pass on to the next generation. The life-cycle hypothesis fits many people's experience quite neatly. It can also accommodate variations. Young couples save to buy a house or flat but when the children arrive, and the wife's earnings may stop for a while, they stop saving, probably for some time.

There is an interesting debate to be had when it comes to housing. Everyday discussion of the economy tends to distinguish between people's investments in financial assets – stocks, bonds, long-term savings accounts – and in housing. The former is often regarded as saving, the latter as consumption. When share prices soar it is a sign of economic health. When house prices do so, it is a sign of danger, of irresponsible behaviour. This distinction between financial and physical assets is, however, hard to sustain. When people buy a house, they are engaging in the household equivalent of a company investing in new factory or office premises. Buying a home, it could be argued, is the ultimate long-term investment, with monthly mortgage payments being the equivalent of a regular savings plan.

Saving behaviour in aggregate both influences and is influenced by what is happening in the wider economy. High unemployment appears to encourage more saving, because people fear they are going to be next to be made redundant. Low inflation seems to be associated with low levels of saving, ideally because individuals have more confidence that the money they have already put aside will not be eaten away by rising prices. It may also be that savers are affected by what is called the 'money illusion'. When inflation is low, interest rates are also usually low, making the rates offered on savings accounts look unattractive. It is of course an illusion. An interest rate of 10 per cent at a time of 8 per cent inflation is lower in real terms (after allowing for inflation) than a 5 per cent rate when inflation is 2 per cent, but such illusions can be surprisingly powerful.

**
*

Many of the basics are now in place. Indeed, we have touched on some fairly sophisticated stuff. We still need to look at what lies behind the behaviour of two other important sets of players – firms and the government – but that will build on what has already been described. First, another entertainment interlude.

6

Classical recipes

When we left Adam Smith, it was with an optimistic view of the
world. As long as economic freedom was maintained, prosperity
would follow. Our next three speakers, all of whom came after
Smith, present a much more mixed vision. The first, Thomas
Robert Malthus (1766–1834), known as Robert Malthus, was
certainly responsible for giving economics its gloomy reputation. It is not clear whether the writer Thomas Carlyle had only
Malthus in mind when describing economics as the 'dismal science', but it is a label that survives to this day in spite of the fact
that most economists are cheery souls. A rather good American
economics website is called www.dismal.com. Also on the bill
are two other great economists from the classical era, mainly the
nineteenth century, David Ricardo (1772–1823) and John Stuart
Mill (1806–73).

Malthusian gloom

Everybody, I suspect, is familiar with the basic ingredients of Malthus's gloomy vision, although most know little about the man who came up with it. Robert Malthus was born into a well-to-do family in Guildford, Surrey, one of eight children. He was blessed not only with intelligence but with sporting ability. He was also good-looking, making the most of it by wearing his hair in long golden curls tinged with pink, a kind of strawberry blond of his day. The effect was rather spoilt when he ventured to speak, a cleft palate he had inherited from his father giving him a high-pitched, whining voice. Malthus excelled in his studies of mathematics and natural philosophy at Cambridge, becoming a fellow of Jesus College before taking holy orders. He gave up his Anglican priesthood in 1804 in order to marry Harriet Eckersal, ten years his junior, although he used the title Reverend in later life, partly to deflect criticism of his views. A year later he took up the post of professor of modern history and political economy at a college established by the East India Company, making him the world's first economics professor (Adam Smith held chairs in logic and moral philosophy), and probably the world's first professional economist.

By then Malthus had already published the first version of the paper that was to make his name. 'An Essay on the Principle of Population, as It Affects the Future Improvement of Society, with Remarks on the Speculations of Mr Godwin, M. Condorcet and Other Writers' is a mouthful, and usually shortened to just 'Essay on Population'. Condorcet, the Marquis de Condorcet (1743–94), was an eighteenth-century French philosopher who had taken Adam Smith's optimistic view of the future and run with it. He saw a future of strongly rising industrial and agricultural production, in which population and living standards would increase together. William Godwin (1756–1836) was born into a strict Calvinist family, trained as a minister, but became a writer and thinker with unconventional views, including regarding marriage as slavery (although he married twice, the first time to the writer Mary Wollstonecraft, who shared his views on marriage – Mary Shelley was their daughter). Godwin also shared Condorcet's optimistic vision of the future and if anything was more utopian in his vision. More importantly, Malthus's father, Daniel, the wealthy Surrey squire, was very taken with Godwin's vision.

The 50,000-word 'Essay on Population' was therefore written by the younger Malthus to settle a family argument, although his father was so impressed he published it at his own expense. The core of Malthus's pessimistic case is contained in just a few sentences of the Essay. He wrote:

I think I may fairly make two postulata. First, that food is necessary to the existence of man. Secondly, that the passion between the sexes is necessary and will remain nearly in its present state. Assuming, then, my postulata as granted, I say that the power of population is indefinitely greater than the power in the earth to produce subsistence for man. Population, when unchecked, increases in geometrical ratio. Subsistence only increases in an arithmetical ratio. A slight acquaintance with the

numbers will show the immensity of the first power in
comparison with the second.

The acquaintance with the numbers he was talking about means that food production, he predicted, would increase arithmetically (2, 4, 6, 8, 10, 12, etc.), while population would rise geometrically (2, 4, 8, 16, 32, 64, etc.). If you have ever owned rabbits, you will get the point. Something had to give, and in Malthus's view the choice was between voluntary restraint on population growth, which he was sceptical about, and something much more nasty, population being controlled by war, pestilence, plague and, perhaps most of all, famine. As for ordinary workers, whom Smith, Condorcet and Godwin had been so optimistic about, Malthus saw their prospects as grim. Workers would not see any rise in living standards; instead they would be stuck at subsistence levels or even below them. Indeed, the sheer grimness of their lives, during periods of which 'the discouragements to marriage and the difficulty of rearing a family are so great', would be one way of keeping population down. Dismal indeed.

Was Malthus wrong?

When I first came across Malthus in the early 1970s, it seemed that, while he might have got his timing wrong, his predictions of a world in which population growth would outstrip food supply chimed in with warnings (which are still around today) that this would be the condition, if it were not already, of much of the Third World. In fact, Malthus got two important things wrong. The first was to underestimate the scope for technological

advance in the production of food and to misunderstand the bio-
logical nature of food production – why should the population of
humans rise geometrically but the population of, say, sheep for
meat eating, rise only arithmetically? Malthus also got the causes
of population growth wrong. Although he wrote on the brink of
a huge increase in world population, from under 1 billion in 1800
to more than 6 billion now, this was not due to lusty peasants
breeding indiscriminately but to medical advances and rising
living standards (including the availability of better and more
plentiful food), which both reduced infant mortality and increased
average life expectancy. The pattern has been for rising living
standards to be associated with smaller, not larger, family size.

Thus, while Third World famine may look like a Malthusian
nightmare, his predictions were too pessimistic. The problem in
developing countries is not that there is a global shortage of food
and they, as the poorest, are missing out. It is that the distribution
of the available food between countries is so uneven. There will
be more on that vexed question towards the end of the book.

Not just population

While Malthus's population predictions may have been wrong,
his contributions on the subject were invaluable. As well as being
the world's first professional economist, he was probably also its
first demographer. Those were not his only claims to fame.
Malthus gave us the 'law of diminishing returns', again derived
from his agricultural observations. There are two ways of looking at this. One is that if ten men work a piece of land they will
get a certain amount of produce out of it. Increasing the number

of workers to twenty will increase the size of the crop but is unlikely to double it because there is only so much the land can produce. The average output per worker falls because after a certain point the *marginal* product of an additional worker – the amount by which he increases output – is smaller than that of the man who came before him. Another way of looking at the same thing is to take the view that most fertile land is already in use at any given time. Raising output would therefore require bringing into play stony, less fertile land, which would produce less. That was why Malthus was gloomy about food production. He may have been wrong on that but the law of diminishing returns was and is an important piece of economics.

Finally, Malthus took on another Frenchman, Jean-Baptiste Say (1767–1832), with another view that went against the opinion of the time. Say, a follower of Adam Smith, said that not only does the market mechanism ensure that supply and demand meet for individual products but that this was true for the economy as a whole. Say's Law, sometimes described as 'supply creates its own demand', or rather that the act of producing goods – paying the wages of workers and so on – will mean there is ready demand for those products. In the aggregate, too, supply will equal demand. General over-production, or glut, was impossible. Malthus disagreed. He saw little danger of glut for essential products such as food. But he thought that over-production was perfectly possible for other goods. So, by extension, was unemployment. Given that unemployment in Britain may have risen to more than a million after the Napoleonic wars, he appears to have had a point. He also had a remedy, advocating 'the employment of the poor in

roads and public works'. In this he was to anticipate John Maynard Keynes, the most famous economist of the twentieth century, by over a hundred years.

David Ricardo

Ricardo, a contemporary of Malthus, has a biography that reads
like that of a character out of Dickens, or perhaps Trollope. One
of a large number of children of a wealthy stockbroker, with
roughly twenty brothers and sisters (the exact number is not
known), he was born in London, a few years after his father, a
Dutch Jew, had left Holland for the City. Ricardo junior appears
to have had an informal education but one that was sufficient to
prepare him for entering the family firm at the age of fourteen.
All went well until, at the age of twenty-one, he fell in love and
married a Quaker girl, thus outside his Jewish faith, a course of
action that was to see him dismissed from the family firm and
disinherited. But Ricardo was clever and resourceful, and he
established his own firm of stockbrokers and built a highly successful business. He was also a man of culture, reading widely,
and in his twenties discovered Smith's *Wealth of Nations* and
began to develop his own approach to economics. By the age of
forty-two, having accumulated enough wealth to retire (he
ranks as the world's richest economist, in a profession that
throws up relatively few millionaires), he had a string of properties, most notably Gatcombe Park in Gloucestershire, the home
of Princess Anne, daughter of the Queen. A few years after
retirement he bought himself a seat in Parliament and was
regarded, unsurprisingly, as the leading expert on economics in

the House of Commons. He did not, however, have much time to develop his political career, dying at the young age of fifty-one.

Ricardo and trade

The bit of Ricardian economics that everybody should know about, and many do, is the law of comparative advantage. Smith argued that the division of labour explained why specialization increased economic output and therefore prosperity. Ricardo developed this, in the setting of international trade, into a fully fledged theory. That countries should specialize in what they are best at seems beyond dispute; it did not need an economist to point this out. But what happens when one country is more efficient than another in everything? Should it produce all those products? And is the other obliged to put up tariff barriers to avoid being swamped with imports from the more efficient country? Ricardo's answer was 'no' on both counts, and he used economic arguments to campaign for free trade in general and the repeal of Britain's nineteenth-century Corn Laws in particular.

The example he used is by now famous. Suppose two countries, England and Portugal, are trading just two products, wine and cloth. Portugal, with the benefit of sunshine, is obviously good at producing wine – it takes twenty-five workers an average of a day's work to produce a barrel. England, in contrast, is inefficient at producing wine, 200 workers being required to produce the same amount, even leaving aside questions of whether it would taste as good. Obviously it is best for Portugal to produce wine. But look too at cloth. In Portugal it also takes twenty-five workers a day to produce a roll of cloth. England is more efficient at producing cloth than wine, but still not as good as Portugal – fifty workers are needed to produce a roll. So what should happen? Portugal has *absolute* advantage in both products. Is the game up for England? Ricardo explained that in these circumstances there would be a net gain in output if Portugal switched production from cloth to wine and England did the opposite. Suppose you start in a situation where, with the same number of workers available in each country, Portugal is producing 1,000 units of wine and 1,000 units of cloth each day. Less efficient England is, by contrast, producing only 500 units of cloth and 125 units of wine. If England switches all its wine workers to cloth production, it will make an extra 500 units of cloth, making 1,000 in all, but no wine. Portugal would in such circumstances produce more wine (to satisfy the English market), and a little less cloth. Its total production of both products would remain at 2,000 units, while England's production would have risen from 625 to 1,000. 'World' output would have gone up. The central point was that what matters in trade is *comparative* advantage, not absolute advantage. Ricardo's law of comparative advantage explains why it is beneficial for countries to trade in every circumstance.

Many people have trouble with this idea. Why should the Portuguese want to buy cloth that is less efficiently produced than their own product? The answer is that the price of English cloth will be determined by 'world' levels. English cloth workers, because they are half as efficient, will tend to be paid half as much as Portuguese workers. The Portuguese will thus be able to afford to buy a significant proportion of the increase in world output. There is still a gain for England and its workers, though, from moving from appallingly inefficient wine production to cloth. It is a 'win–win' situation.

Ricardo and economics

Although the law of comparative advantage stands as Ricardo's most enduring contribution, there was much more to his economics than that. Because of his expertise in finance, he was the first to take the subject beyond the polemic, 'political economy' approach of his day and into areas both more abstract and more scientific. With his complex ideas and ready intelligence, Ricardo was the first to introduce difficult mathematical concepts into the subject – a move that some say started the rot. Anybody trying to understand an equation-filled academic paper on economics today should perhaps blame Ricardo.

While the law of comparative advantage offered an upbeat assessment of the gains from trade, much of Ricardo's vision, like that of his friend Malthus, was gloomy. He helped develop the law of diminishing returns, and like Malthus he also had a pessimistic view of the future. Ricardo's 'corn model' was concerned with how wealth was distributed, not how it was created. In an approach that was to provide Marx with the basis of his economic theories, Ricardo saw the battle over the distribution of the economic cake as more important than the size of the cake itself. Income would be divided between wages, profits and landlords' rents. If wages rose, profits would fall, and vice versa.

In the long run, he suggested, landlords would be likely to gain at the expense of workers, whose wages would not rise much above subsistence level, and profits, which would be insufficient to encourage investment in new production. As a result, it was hard to be optimistic about long-term economic prospects.

Finally, Ricardo also gave us an approach that has gained favour in recent times. For years economists have puzzled about why, after Japan's 'bubble economy' burst in the late 1980s, successive efforts by the Japanese government to boost the economy through tax cuts and extra public spending have failed. The answer, developed by modern-day American economists such as Robert Barro, is that such measures have no effect because people know they will have to pay for them later in higher taxes. An increase in the budget deficit is exactly matched by a rise in the surplus of the private sector. Because Ricardo suggested something similar, this is known as Ricardian equivalence. The classical economists, it seems, still have a great deal of relevance.

John Stuart Mill

John Stuart Mill, who has been described as the most important liberal thinker of the nineteenth century, is often not thought of as an economist at all. His greatest book, *On Liberty*, was a work of philosophy. There is a question of how much of an original thinker, and how much of an interpreter and popularizer Mill was on economics. Perhaps it was just a matter of timing. His *Principles of Political Economy*, published in 1848, was the standard text on the subject for nearly half a century.

Mill was always destined for great things. His father, James, was a well-known political economist and the Mill household regularly played host to Jeremy Bentham and David Ricardo, friends and mentors. It was an intellectual hothouse that, he reflected later in life, gave him a twenty-five-year head start on his contemporaries. The younger Mill was reading the classics in their original Greek at the age of eight, by which time he was already familiar with Latin. He began to study economics at thirteen and in his late teens edited Bentham's writings into a five-volume collection, *On Evidence*, for which effort he suffered a nervous breakdown. Bentham, whose embalmed body is usually on display in the main entrance hall at University College London, the result of a bizarre stipulation in his will (although at the time of writing it was away for some repairs), was famous for 'utilitarianism'. This sounds more forbidding than it need be. At its most basic, utility is merely usefulness. Used in the sense Bentham intended, however, it is, more than that, a way of expressing pleasure, happiness and satisfaction. And the principle of Bentham's utilitarianism was 'the greatest happiness for the greatest number'. It is easy to see how that principle still applies. When a new public project such as Terminal Five at Heathrow is planned, it is customary to conduct a cost–benefit analysis – if the benefits exceed the costs the 'greatest happiness' is achieved and the project goes ahead. If not it is abandoned. After the Chancellor unveils his Budget proposals each spring, there is always analysis of the 'winners and losers'. Any Chancellor aiming for a long political life will always ensure the former exceed the latter. Later economists were to develop the Bentham–Mill framework into an entire field of the subject – welfare economics. Economists refer to a 'Pareto' optimal situation, after the French-born economist Vilfredo Pareto (1848–1923). This is a situation in which nobody can be made better off without making others worse off.

Mill built on this utilitarian tradition in his work (he soon got over his nervous breakdown and joined his father working for the East India Company, which seemed to offer plenty of opportunity for freelance thinking and writing). Apart from a slightly odd view about economic growth – he thought the industrial revolution was just a temporary interlude after which the economy would return to a 'stationary state' – his great contribution was in demonstrating that while economic laws applied in certain areas, they did not in others. 'The laws and conditions of the production of wealth partake of the character of physical truths,' he wrote. 'There is nothing optional or arbitrary in them. It is not so with the distribution of wealth. That is a matter of human institution solely.'

How much was produced in an economy, in other words, was determined by economic laws. But there were no laws that set down how the wealth so created should be distributed among the population. This was new. Mill, taking Ricardo's line that, unchecked, most wealth was likely to find its way to landlords, was unhappy even with the idea of private property. Most of all he thought that society could arrange the distribution of wealth in a way that would bring the greatest happiness to the greatest number. In this he was a 'utopian' socialist. Socialists seeking fairer shares for all took his analysis up more generally.

7

Cordon bleu business

As we have looked at how consumers go about deciding what and how much to buy, and how the various components of gross domestic product fit together, it has so far been taken for granted that firms will always be willing to supply goods and services. That is not a bad description of the way things are. In real life there is always somebody willing to meet the needs of customers, to fill a 'gap in the market'. Adam Smith's 'the butcher, the brewer and the baker' are driven to provide us with meat, beer and bread by the prospect of making money — and if they did not, somebody else would. If we were not sitting in this particular restaurant there would surely be another, owned by different people, but probably every bit as good. In many instances, firms will themselves create the market through new products,

advertising and promotion. That is the way the capital
keeps ticking over. That observation does not, however, help
much in terms of explaining what makes businesses function,
how they go about deciding how much to invest, how much to
produce and at what price. Perhaps we should start by asking a
very basic question. Why do we have firms at all?

Companies and individuals

We consume as individuals, or families, so why don't we produce in the same way? Actually, many of us do. There are about
3 million self-employed people in Britain, effectively one-man
or one-woman businesses, including everything from plumbers
and electricians through to IT contractors, journalists and top
entertainers. The process by which businesses grow can easily be
seen if we start with a one-man business. John the builder begins
on his own, putting up garden walls. Soon somebody, impressed
with his work, asks him to build a house extension. He is happy
to do so but needs to take on a couple of staff. The job is successful and more orders result. Soon he has three house exten-
sions on the go at the same time. Not only does he take on more
workers but he effectively becomes the manager, supervising all
three projects but doing much less of the building work himself.
A contract to build a house follows, then another. Then, with
the help of the bank and one or two friends with money to
invest, he buys a plot of land to turn into a housing development. Now he does not just employ builders but accountants
and marketing people. A few years down the road and John has
become a public limited company, a plc, quoted on the Stock

g developments across the country,
gone.

their history in something like that way.
an businesses, of course, remain happily in
are many more self-employed people than firms
em   others, and there are roughly ten times as many
employees as there are self-employed people. Some self-
employed people eventually opt for what they see as the security
of employment. The majority of people work for somebody
else, whether it is a firm or a public sector organization. To find
the reason for this, we need look no further than Adam Smith.
He explained, with the example of the pin factory, how specialization, the division of labour, increased efficiency and thus dramatically lowered costs. A sole trader could still produce pins but
would be unable to compete on price with the factory. That is
why many self-employed people and very small businesses
emphasize the special or bespoke nature of their service – you
pay more but you get something better, or at least more individual. In many cases production is simply outside the scope of
an individual. Much as I would love to write, edit, design and
print a national newspaper, it is not a task that can be undertaken
by one person. The fact that there are certain minimum person-
nel requirements in many areas of production, and in quite a lot
of service industries, does not necessarily mean that people have
to be organized into what we usually think of as a firm, with an
owner-manager, or with managers and outside shareholders.
Journalists and printers could, for example, organize themselves
as a collective. There are partnerships and member-owned

mutual organizations, such as the traditional British building society, although they are a dying breed. The John Lewis Partnership, a very successful retailer, is owned by its employees. Even so, it is useful to think of firms in the conventional way and of their main motivation being that of generating profits.

Counting costs

The costs of running a business are easy enough to determine and consist of wages, raw materials and components, power, distribution (getting the goods to customers) and rent. There is also the cost of investment, expressed in terms of 'depreciation'. If a business buys a computer costing £1,000 and it is reckoned to have a five-year life, its annual cost averages out at £200. It depreciates in value by £200 every year until, by the end of five years, it is worth nothing. It is usual to split the costs faced by a firm into 'fixed' and 'variable'. Fixed costs will include those of buildings and of equipment already bought. Variable costs include wages, which vary according to the number of people employed and the hours they work (although in many companies the basic salaries of permanent staff are effectively a fixed cost). Other variable costs include those for materials and components, energy use and distribution. Variable costs rise in direct proportion to the amount produced, unlike fixed costs. The bigger the output of the firm, the smaller the amount of fixed costs for each unit produced. The costs for every car produced of the premises in which they are made go down as the rent for the factory is divided among a larger output. Fixed costs per unit of output start rising only if production gets to a level where the original factory is not big enough and a new one has to be acquired.

Spreading fixed costs over a larger amount of output is one of the most important sources of *economies of scale*, the tendency for the cost per unit to fall as output rises. Big firms can do things more cheaply than small firms. Assembly-line cars are cheaper, even if they do not have the same cachet, than hand-made ones, because the more specialized a task – for example fitting the hubcaps on a car – the more efficient an individual worker becomes at doing it. There are other sources of economies of scale – a full lorry does not cost much more to run than a half-full one, but the full one's costs are spread across twice the amount of goods. Management costs, and those of advertising, are similarly spread over a larger amount of output. This process does not, however, continue indefinitely, or else the ideal situation in every industry would be one giant firm, a monopoly.

Diseconomies of scale, rising unit costs, also apply after a certain point. One would be the cost of acquiring another factory, described above, although if the new factory quickly became employed to full capacity that would soon pass. Another would be the tendency, above a certain size of company, for lean and efficient management to be replaced by layers of bureaucracy. A growing firm will also have to look further afield for its customers. Transport costs may rise and markets become more distant from the source of production. Wage costs may rise, because the pool of workers with the right skills is used up and because big firms are more likely to be unionized.

Making profits

Why do firms aim to make profits? While there is a body of literature that says managers are motivated by a range of things –
the size of the firm, or their part of it, the size of their office, the
size of their company car, even the attractiveness of their secretary (which can apply equally to male and female managers) –
profit is at the root of it. Without profit, why should anybody set
up in business, when a more lucrative and less stressful life would
be available working for somebody else? And why would any
investor put cash into a business that makes no money, when it
could generate a safe return in the bank? It is not, perhaps, as
clear-cut as that. Many people set up in business because the
option of paid employment is closed off to them. Think, for
example, of former bankers, clutching redundancy cheques,
who fulfil their lifetime ambition to open a restaurant. The failure rate of such ventures, not surprisingly, is quite high. As for
investors and profits, the willingness of people in the second half
of the 1990s to put money into dot.com firms that were not
making money, and had little hope of doing so, appeared to give
the lie to the view that investors are interested only in profitable
companies. Then again, investors would doubtless have said they
were investing, not on the basis of current profits but because of
future potential. They probably also believed that, because they
spotted that potential sooner than everybody else, there would
be every opportunity to make substantial capital gains on their
shares.

Leaving such quibbles aside, the textbook aim of firms is to
maximize profits. It is also, pretty much, the real-world aim.

This seems simple enough. 'Annual income twenty pounds, annual expenditure nineteen nineteen six, result happiness,' said Dickens's Mr Micawber. 'Annual income twenty pounds, annual expenditure twenty pounds nought and six, result misery.' But, while Dickens pointed out that being in the black is better than being in the red, there is a little more to it than that. Fortunately, economists can help. They can explain to firms how to maximize their profits, and it is surprisingly simple. To do so, we need just two tools.

The first is concerned with expenditure, or costs, the second with income, or revenue. The idea that costs vary with the amount produced has already been touched upon. Fixed costs tend to fall per unit of output as production increases. Variable costs are likely to rise in proportion to output but may then start to increase faster. For example, it is necessary to pay workers overtime rates, higher than basic pay, to increase output above a certain level. At every level of output it will be possible to calculate the *marginal* cost – the cost of producing one extra unit. A typical pattern would be that marginal cost will tend to fall up to a certain level, so that it costs less and less to produce each extra unit, but then begin to rise. Marginal cost, then, is our first essential tool.

The other is marginal revenue, its direct counterpart on the income side of the firm's accounts. Just as it is possible to calculate marginal cost, so the same can be done for revenue. Marginal revenue is simply the extra revenue, at any point, from an additional sale. Think, say, of new season winter clothing. A few fashion victims will buy it as soon as hits the stores, in August or early September. Many others will wait until the mid-season sale in October or November, when prices are first cut. Plenty more will hold on until the January sales, when they are cut further. Finally, some who care nothing of fashion will buy in the spring at a factory outlet sale at rock bottom prices. Each time the marginal revenue, the income from each extra sale, declines.

So how do you know how much to make to maximize profit? The answer is not only easy but it is also, unlike some economics, sound common sense. You stop increasing production when you are on the point of losing money on any extra sales. You do not, in other words, sell anything at a loss. As long as the extra revenue from an additional sale exceeds the cost to you of generating that sale, carry on raising output. Once the extra revenue merely equals your additional cost – marginal revenue equals marginal cost – it is time to call a halt. Actually, this is easier than it sounds for most businesses. The example of the clothing firm is one in which the price varies and the firm controls how much it varies over time. For most companies that does not occur. The market – the collective decisions of competitors and consumers – determines the price. Marginal revenue (price) remains the same. All that is necessary is to ensure that output does not rise above the point where marginal cost is equal to that price. Any further increases in output will mean that you are subsidizing customers by selling at a loss. You can make this point with diagrams but I do not want to make this look like a textbook. For those who are curious, most textbooks will provide a picture.

Let me just clarify one thing that puzzles a lot of people. By increasing production to the point where marginal revenue merely equals marginal cost firms are still making profits. This is because before they get to that point they will have made many sales where marginal revenue exceeds marginal cost, probably by a substantial amount. By producing to the point where there is no additional profit, they are ensuring they have squeezed every bit of profit out of the market they are in.

Do businesses actually behave like this?

I have met very many business people over the years, some excellent and others not so good. The better ones, incidentally, are usually pretty hot on economics. The mediocre ones tend to converse in some kind of horrible management-speak, talking of 'growing the business', 're-engineering', 'low hanging fruit' and the rest. But, good or bad, I cannot recall a single businessman telling me that his aim in life was to make sure his marginal revenue equalled his marginal cost. There are a few reasons for this. One is that economics has to try to simplify a complicated real world. Businesses will operate a number of strategies, for example deliberately selling at a loss over a number of months or years in order to build market share and drive out competitors. Such strategies are easier, of course, if the business can draw on financial support from another part of the operation. Or, to take another example, supermarket chains often sell certain goods, so-called 'known-value' items such as bread and milk, below marginal cost, in the knowledge that they can recoup the lost profits elsewhere, in products where consumers are less aware of the prices. Another reason is that not all businesses maximize profits, even when they think they are doing so.

The fact is that matching marginal cost and marginal revenue is one of the building blocks of business, even if it is implicit in the decisions businesses make rather than explicitly stated. The clothes retailer in the example above knows fairly precisely the prices he or she needs to be able to achieve at various times during the selling season in order to maximize profit. The retailer also knows that things can occur in real life that complicate the task. A mild autumn, for example, when few people buy winter clothes, would make it very hard to maximize profit. These complications aside, in the end businesses that ignore the economic rules will not survive long.

Theory and practice come together in areas such as economies of scale, which provided the rationale for mass production, for Henry Ford's assembly lines, and therefore for industrial development in the twentieth century. Perhaps the best example where theory and practice come together, however, is in the field of competition. It is a rather interesting area.

Playing the monopoly game

When Britain's Labour government was elected in May 1997, it promised many things. In the economic sphere, however, under Gordon Brown it was able to deliver a three-pronged reform of the economic policy framework. The first was to give operational independence – control over interest rates – to the Bank of England. The second was to put in place rules for the conduct of fiscal policy, tax and spending, of which more later. The third, which took the Treasury into an area usually thought of as

the preserve of the Department of Trade and Industry, was a significant beefing-up of competition, or anti-monopoly, policy.
The powers and resources of the competition authorities, the
Competition Commission (the old Monopolies and Mergers
Commission) and the Office of Fair Trading, were strengthened.
The OFT, in effect the country's competition watchdog, was
given the power not only to initiate investigations but also to
fine companies it suspects of stitching-up the market – running
cartels – up to 10 per cent of their turnover, and to prosecute,
with the threat of imprisonment, directors who obstruct its
investigations. Some of this was influenced by America, where
tough anti-trust laws have been in place for decades. There has
also been a strengthening of EU-wide competition regime.

It remains to be seen how successful this approach, criticized
by the business lobby as draconian, turns out to be. There were
two reasons, however, why the government was keen to crack
down on monopolies. The first was that it believed they acted to
the detriment of consumers, charging them higher prices than
would be the case if many companies were competing for
custom. The second was that lack of competition was seen to be
damaging in another way. Competition, ministers and officials
said, was vital for economic efficiency. Monopolies, because
they have the market to themselves, can become bloated and
inefficient. This, in turn, affects the country's ability to compete
with others, the nation's 'competitiveness'. As an aside, you will
have noticed by now that there is a tendency in economics for
similar words to have quite different meanings. In this case,
competition refers to the extent to which different firms are able

to compete for business in a particular market. A contestable market, to introduce another term, is one in which it is easy for firms to enter (or leave). Competitiveness means the ability of one country's economy (or the individuals and firms than make up that economy) to compete with others.

Why is lack of competition, monopoly, bad for consumers? After all, if economies of scale are involved to any degree, will it not be the case that bigger is cheaper? Ford, which would doubtless love to have a complete monopoly of the car market, could claim that adding to its already very long production runs would bring down the cost of each car produced. It would also save on the vast amounts of advertising it employs to try to convince customers its products are better than those of General Motors, Toyota or Fiat. A benign monopolist would surely give us the best of all worlds.

The problem, apart from the fact that the idea of a benign monopolist is probably a contradiction in terms, is that it would not be the best of all worlds, by a long way. For one thing it would deprive consumers of choice, and choice is in itself a significant benefit. More importantly, monopoly is likely to mean higher prices. Why is this? The best way of thinking about it is to compare two extremes. One is 'perfect' competition, a situation in which very many firms compete in an industry, each producing identical products, and none big enough to influence the price with its behaviour. Each firm produces to the point where its marginal cost equals marginal revenue, so this is also the situation for the industry as a whole. Each firm has to accept the price set by the market and that price, by the magic of competition, not only maximizes the profit of each individual firm but it is also lower than would be charged by any monopolist.

This is because the monopolist, in contrast, can influence prices. Let us suppose that Ford, which we assume for these purposes is the sole supplier to the UK car market, could sell one million cars a year at £10,000 each but two million at a price of £5,000. It cannot, by the way, sell the first million at £10,000 and the second at £5,000 because it would not be acceptable to the first million customers. The more the company supplies, the lower the price it gets. The monopolist's demand curve (the lower the price the more customers will want to buy) is the same as that for the industry as a whole. He, in other words, is the industry. So what does the monopolist do? What he does is simply follow the standard rule, by also producing to where his marginal cost and revenue are equal. The monopolist, however, is unusual: the extra revenue he gets from selling, say, an additional car, has to take into account the fact that producing more in a given period will lower prices across the board. This is easy to demonstrate. Say Ford worked out that it could sell 1,000 cars at a price of £10,000, but to sell 1,001 the price has to drop to £9,999. The marginal revenue from the 1,001st is, in effect, £9,999 less £1,000, £8,999. Why? Because the £1 price cut on the 1,001st also has to apply to the first 1,000 off the production line but not yet sold.

Two things result from this. The first is that a monopolist will produce less than would be the case in a perfectly competitive market with lots of firms fighting for their share. The second is that prices will be higher. For the perfectly competitive firm, marginal revenue is equal to the price in the market. For the monopolist, price – in this case £9,999 – is higher than marginal revenue (£8,999), and he is able to make 'supernormal' or monopoly profits. This is why monopolies are bad for consumers.

Real-world competition

Textbook ideas of competition and the real world are rather different. There are very few cases of firms being so powerful and dominant that they can maintain a permanent monopoly position in which barriers to entry are so formidable that potential competitors are permanently deterred from trying to take them on. There are plenty of examples of temporary monopolies, such as when a company has developed an entirely new product, particularly when it is protected by patent. Typically though, such monopolies do not last, even with patents. The makers of the Rubik cube, an immensely popular puzzle, enjoyed a brief and hugely profitable monopoly in the 1980s before competitors and black-market copiers moved in. So did Laszlo Biró, who in 1938 invented and marketed the first ballpoint pen. We may still often call such pens 'Biros' but the market in them is no monopoly, in fact it is highly competitive. Some monopolies do, however, survive. So do plenty of examples of oligopolies – industries where there are just a small number of competitors, perhaps four or five.

In Britain it is common to talk of the Big Four high street banks – currently HSBC, Lloyds-TSB, Barclays and Royal Bank of Scotland (which acquired National Westminster, previously a big four bank). In food retailing, too, it is common to talk of the Big Four – Tesco, Sainsbury, ASDA and Safeway. Both sectors have been the subject of regular investigations by the competition authorities to try to detect whether they are engaged in collusive, or cartel-like, behaviour. A cartel is when a group of firms, big enough to dominate the market, plot together so that they collectively act as a monopoly, setting higher prices and achieving monopoly profits. On its website, the OFT offers immunity from prosecution to people who inform on companies they suspect of engaging in cartel activity. Anti-competitive behaviour does not necessarily involve cartel activity. In 2001, for example, the OFT successfully pushed through a change which significantly reduced the prices of over-the-counter medicines. In that case, while high prices were benefiting the pharmaceutical companies, they existed because, thirty years earlier small chemists had persuaded the government that resale price maintenance (the fixing of prices by the manufacturers) should be allowed to prevent them being driven out of business by the bigger pharmacy chains. The OFT's view was that this was a restrictive practice that acted against the interests of consumers.

When it comes to cartels, the real-world example most people think of is the Organisation of Petroleum Exporting Countries, OPEC, which has in the past successfully restricted output in order to raise world oil prices, most dramatically in 1973–4 and 1979–80. There is, however, a question about whether OPEC, which controls about 40 per cent of world oil supplies, has a sufficiently dominant position to act as a true cartel. In recent years it has relied on the co-operation of non-

OPEC oil producers to achieve its aims. Experts predict, perhaps worryingly, that OPEC's dominance of world oil supplies will increase significantly during the twenty-first century.

Monopolies and privatization

One of the problems economists have with monopolies is that there is often a trade-off between the efficiency that can arise from having one large supplier, most notably economies of scale, and the risk, indeed the likelihood, that monopolies will exploit their position. What happens, for example, if the optimum size of an industry, in terms of efficiency, is just one big firm? What happens if there is a 'natural' monopoly? In Britain the traditional response to this problem was to accept the argument that there were certain natural monopolies, or at least sectors where competition was wasteful and inefficient. What purpose could be served, it was argued, from having two companies competing to send gas along adjacent pipelines to supply homes, factories or offices? Or two or more sets of electricity cables? The solution, therefore, was to allow monopolies in these areas but bring them under public ownership in order to ensure they did not make excessive profits. Many of Britain's nationalized industries, most brought into public ownership by the 1945–51 Labour government, were monopolies. But, being controlled, they did not make profits at the expense of the consumer. Many, in fact, did not make profits at all.

The existence of public sector monopolies, in gas, electricity, water, coal, rail, telecommunications and other areas, created a problem for the Conservative government when it wanted to privatize them in the 1980s. On the one hand, their monopoly status made them highly attractive to investors with an eye on the potential profits these industries could make once transferred to the private sector. On the other, there was a risk of creating Frankenstein's monsters – great bloated but enormously profitable firms, dominating the supply of essential services. The approach to this problem evolved over time. British Telecom, in which the government in 1984 first sold shares, was transferred to the private sector as a monopoly. It was given its own regulator, Oftel, vital to oversee the conduct of such a huge monopoly, but the regulatory regime for the first few years was a loose one. Investors made a lot of money. Gradually, through the privatizations of gas, electricity and water, a more sophisticated approach evolved, allowing enough in terms of potential profit to achieve a successful sell-off but introducing stiffer competition at an earlier stage. By the time the government privatized British Rail in 1996, it believed the process had evolved enough to allow competition from day one. Thus, the nationalized British Rail was broken up into three broad segments, one company with responsibility for the track, signalling, stations and land, Railtrack; a whole series of train-operating companies running different services; and rolling-stock leasing companies, which took on BR's locomotives, carriages and trucks and leased them to the operating companies. The result was not only the instant break-up of a monopoly but, many would say, a fragmentation that led to many of the subsequent problems of the railways, including the failure of Railtrack, culminating in the Labour government's decision to put it into administration in

October 2001. Monopoly can be bad, but you have to take care when dismantling it. Indeed, the debate over rail privatization raises questions of whether the nationalized industry was a natural monopoly and whether a better solution would have been to invest more money in it while maintaining public ownership.

Is the Internet perfect competition?

When the dot.com revolution happened in the second half of the 1990s industry analysts predicted an explosion in online retailing, or B2C (business-to-consumer) sales, as well as a big increase in B2B (business-to-business) and B2G (business-to-government) activity – there are probably many more of these acronyms but that is enough. Economists, meanwhile, asked a rather different question. Was the Internet a real-world example of the perfectly competitive market of the textbooks? Its claims to be so were rather good. For one thing, the barriers to entry in the vast majority of online markets appeared to be very low. Anybody could set themselves up as an e-tailer of, say, books or compact discs, as long as they could buy such products wholesale from the publishers or manufacturers and could take on a few people to pack them up and send them off to customers. Compared with the cost of establishing a nationwide network of shops to take on WHSmith, Our Price or Virgin, even a state-of-the-art website required only a small outlay. If one requirement of perfect competition is that there are many competitors, the Internet also fulfilled another. One source of monopoly pricing, for any product, is the lack of information available to customers. I can sell you a CD for £15 as long as you are unaware that a few miles away somebody is selling it for £12. To make you aware, my competitor would have to advertise, which would increase his costs. Even then, you might decide it is not worth the journey.

The Internet can provide something like perfect information. It has, in fact, spawned the growth of websites whose specific task is to check prices. These sites are not always comprehensive but they do provide something close to price transparency. It is possible in a few seconds to see who is offering the best deal on a product. Add in the fact that geography is far less important – even for people who confine their online shopping to UK sites there is usually no difference in shipping costs whether the supplier is a few miles or several hundred miles away – and the Internet does indeed start to look like the perfect competition of the textbooks.

So why is it not turning out that way? Online retailing may not yet have grown as rapidly as its most optimistic proponents hoped but its impact has been significant. Bricks and mortar retailers, apart from running their own e-tailing sites, have had to take account of the prices available online when setting their prices in the shops. The Internet has thus been a force for low inflation, and has helped bring about falling prices for many goods. It has not yet, however, resulted in perfect competition. Only a minority of online shoppers use price-checking sites (usually free to the customer) before deciding on a purchase. The information is there but most customers are not making use of it. Those who do not, and even some who do, are still heavily influenced by reputation. They will buy from online retailers they have heard of and who they trust not to make off with their credit card details. Simply setting up a website is unlikely to be enough to build a strong market position. A good reputation is also required. How do e-tailers go about building reputation? By spending a lot on advertising. Existing retailers start with an advantage in that their names are already known. Those seeking to sell online have to get their name across in another way. Think of the amount of advertising by Amazon, or in Britain a company like lastminute.com during the height of the dot.com boom, and you get the point. Amazon's strategy was to erect a barrier to entry by convincing the public, through heavy advertising, that it was *the* books e-tailer. To a large extent it appears to have worked. In place of the barrier to entry of the cost of establishing a network of stores, a new one emerged – the need for advertising budgets stretching into tens of millions. Perhaps this will change again, and the growing sophistication of online shoppers will give us something like a perfect market. But it is not there yet.

What about companies that do not sell a product but a 'weightless' service? What about online businesses whose product is, say, music tracks or movies that can be downloaded over the Internet? This is an interesting area. Most of the above principles apply. Such services may be weightless but they are not costless. An online music provider, for example, has to invest in web capacity – the greater the demand the bigger the capacity – and in marketing and administration. The economies of scale can be considerable but there are still marginal costs and revenues. It does, however, mean that such markets can be truly global. Thinking of mail delivery times and reliability you might not want to buy CDs from a site based in Bombay, Shanghai or Sacramento. That does not apply if the product is simply downloaded.

Business games

The approach that firms took in the online market is an example of a business strategy. Economists in the twentieth century took an increasing interest in such strategies as real-world examples of 'game theory'. The idea of game theory is simple. Whether you gain maximum advantage in a particular situation depends not just on what you do but on what others do. Amazon's decision to spend so much promoting its name was influenced in part by its expectations of what others, including the existing book retailers, would do. Do I open a new supermarket in a particular part of town? Perhaps, but to determine how profitable it is likely to be I would also want to know whether others are planning to do so. Many students are introduced to game theory in the form of the prisoner's dilemma, in which two suspects are questioned about an offence. The obvious strategy for each of them is to plead innocent but rat on the other one. If both do so, though, the authorities are likely to deem them both guilty and give them an extra sentence for dishonesty. Depending on what the other does, the optimum strategy for each individual could be to plead either guilty or innocent, but to know which is best he has to form a judgement on what the other will do. In a market of two firms, the best collusive strategy would be for them both to restrict output so as to keep prices high. But if one firm restricts its output while the other pumps out as much as it can, the first firm would be a loser. Guessing, or finding out, what your competitor is up to is all part of the game.

Game theory has attracted some eccentric economists. Paul Strathern called his book *Dr Strangelove's Game* after John Von Neumann, who, together with his colleague Oskar Morgenstern, effectively invented game theory and gave us the 'zero-sum game' – one player's gain is another's loss. It was the Hungarian-born Von Neumann, a man with an extraordinary sex drive, who, in the 1950s and by this time confined to a wheelchair, advised the American government on its Cold War strategy in relation to the Soviet Union, based on a game theory approach. In this case, while the best outcome for America might have been to blow up Moscow with no retaliation, 'mutually assured destruction' was the chosen alternative. John Nash, the brilliant American game theorist who developed the idea of the 'Nash equilibrium' – the optimum solution for all players in any game – became a shambling drop-out in the 1970s and 1980s after suffering bouts of schizophrenia but recovered sufficiently to be awarded the Nobel Prize for economics in 1994. Nash took game theory on by demonstrating the possibility of 'win–win' outcomes, in which all players could gain. He was the subject of an award-winning film in 2001, *A Beautiful Mind*, in which Russell Crowe narrowly missed out on an Oscar for his performance as Nash.

Governments have tried to use game theory in devising ways of allocating licences, for example for oil exploration, to busi-

nesses. One of the most interesting examples of the practical use
of game theory in a business context came in Britain in 2000
when the government held an auction for third-generation (3G)
mobile telephone licences. In designing the auction, the government called on the services of a team of economists specializing
in game theory, led by Professor Ken Binmore of the University
of London. The design they came up with was no ivory tower
creation. For nearly two years, using research students as 'players', the team tried different approaches to determine how the
bidders were likely to respond under various conditions. For the
telecom firms bidding for licences, the best outcome would have
been that each paid a small amount for the licences on offer but
that depended on awareness of how the others would bid. In the
event, this battle of the game theorists (the bidding companies
also employed their own) turned into a comprehensive victory
for the government side. Helped by timing, the stock market's
mobile telephone frenzy being at its height, the auction raised
the extraordinary sum of £22.47 billion, enough to build 400
new hospitals and many times the sum expected at the start of
the process. Within a few weeks, as the telecom bubble burst,
the companies were asking for their money back. The fact was
that the bidders misjudged their game theory very badly. Even
the biggest firms would have done better to hold back when the
bidding got out of hand. As Binmore later put it:

> *Nobody is forced to bid in an auction, and anybody who bids
> more for a licence than he thinks it is worth is just plain stupid.
> Claims that the complexity of the auction led the bidders astray*

*do not stand up to serious scrutiny. In our auction, the optimal
strategy was absurdly simple: just make the minimum bid for
whichever licence would maximize your profit if you won it at
that price.*

Why firms invest

Bidding in a licence auction is one way in which firms invest,
albeit an unusual one. It raises more general questions. Why do
firms invest, and what determines the amount they invest? For
decades, one of the supposed weaknesses of Britain's economy
was under-investment – spending a smaller proportion of GDP
on investment than rival economies. Lately, the Treasury has
produced figures suggesting that business investment, at about
15 per cent of GDP, is similar to that of the other Group of
Seven (America, Japan, Germany, Britain, France, Italy and
Canada) industrial countries. The legacy of past under-investment remains, however, with the capital stock per worker (the
amount of equipment available, for example) some 30 per cent
higher in America, 40 per cent higher in France and 50 per cent
higher in Germany, than in Britain. Why is this important?
Because, as the Treasury puts it:

*A high quantity and quality of investment has two key
influences. The first is that it increases the level of inputs into the
economy – increasing the productivity and hence the earnings of
workers in a very direct way. But it is also a vital channel for the
introduction of new technology and processes. New investment*

does not just replace existing machinery, but moves forward production processes by embodying technical change.

Investment by businesses is not, of course, the only source of capital expenditure. Economists would argue that under-investment by government in the infrastructure – roads, railways, hospitals and schools – has been as serious as the legacy of business under-investment. Leaving that aside for later, it is clear that a vital ingredient in the long-term success of any economy is an adequate level of investment. It is also essential for the long-term health of any company. But what determines how much firms are prepared to invest? On the face of it, the reasons for company investment are as many and as complex as those that determine why we choose on a particular day to buy something in the shops. Managers might decide to invest to replace a noisy or worn-out piece of machinery or vehicle. They might, similarly, decide to replace all the firm's personal computers because they are becoming obsolete. It could be that the firm has decided on a new product range and needs to invest in new equipment to produce it. Or, perhaps, the company has been doing well, is flush with cash, and decides to spend some of it.

In fact, while all these are subsidiary reasons why firms may decide to invest, there is one easy underlying explanation. Investment will occur when it is expected to generate a sufficient rate of return. A new piece of equipment, in other words, not only has to pay for itself in what it adds to revenue and profit, but it has to generate a return over and above this. How high does that return have to be? That depends on the alternatives. Suppose the level of interest rates is 10 per cent and the cost of a new industrial plant is £10 million. If the firm already has cash of £10 million, it could invest it in the new plant, or it could simply leave the money in the bank, where it will generate a 10 per cent return, equivalent to £1 million in the first year and more, if no money is withdrawn and the value of the deposit grows, in subsequent years. To make the investment worth making, its rate of return has to exceed 10 per cent, probably by a comfortable margin. So the income of the firm as a result of the new investment will have to rise by more than £1 million in the first year, and so on. Economists call this alternative use the 'opportunity cost' of the investment – the return that would have been available if the cash invested had been put to its next best use. The same principle applies if the firm has to borrow the money from the bank. Again that borrowing will not be worthwhile if the investment does not generate a return significantly higher than the cost of the funds.

This explains why high interest rates, and in particular high 'real' rates of interest (the interest rate after allowing for inflation – a 15 per cent interest rate with 10 per cent inflation is a 5 per cent real interest rate) tend to discourage investment. Low and stable interest rates are likely to be more conducive to investment. Of course, when it comes to assessing the return on an investment, accountants may struggle to be as precise as economists would like. In the absence of a controlled experiment, could a firm possibly tell exactly what the rate of return is on an investment in ten £2,000 computers, and how it would differ if twelve had been bought? Probably not, but the same general point applies as with marginal cost and revenue, discussed above. Firms that ignore such rules will eventually get into trouble. Managers who invest willy-nilly, without regard for the rate of return, should not expect a very long career in business.

Should firms have a conscience?

One of the interesting developments in recent years has been the recognition by companies that there is much more to corporate life than money. Corporate social responsibility, the idea that it is 'not just profit', is not new in itself. Andrew Carnegie (1835–1919), the Scottish-born American industrialist, is famous for endowing a high proportion of the public libraries in Britain, as well as the Carnegie Institute of Technology, the Carnegie Institution and the Carnegie Hall in America. The Cadbury family in Birmingham was a notable early example of the enlightened company, both in the treatment of its workers – taking them from the slums of the city to work and live among the green fields, back then at least, of Bourneville. They were not the only ones. When religion and business mixed – the Cadburys were Quakers – greater attention to the social obligations of commerce was often the result.

Firms would say they have always taken such obligations seriously. Happy and healthy employees are likely to be more productive. Customers will be more likely to buy from firms that are regarded as good corporate citizens – not polluting the environment or exploiting Third World suppliers, for example. Money spent on community projects or charitable work has the useful side effect, perhaps even the main effect, of generating a warm image for the business. In recent years, however, such matters have climbed higher up the corporate agenda. Businessmen have become more fearful of the actions of pressure groups, whether they be anti-globalization protestors capable of disrupting business gatherings or annual general meetings, or environmental charities. When Greenpeace successfully lobbied Shell against the dumping of the Brent Spar oil platform in deep ocean waters, doing so by creating a consumer boycott of the company's products, it was a watershed. The fact that Greenpeace was subsequently shown to have got its facts wrong over the environmental effects of Shell's original plan seemed to matter less than the power it had demonstrated to exert influence over company actions.

One popular way of looking at this is through the 'stakeholder' model. In this, the owners of the company, the shareholders, are important but they have to take their place alongside others. Thus, there are internal stakeholders in the business – the shareholders plus the managers and workers – but there are also 'external' stakeholders. These include customers and suppliers, but they also include competitors. How so? One company, if it produced shoddy products, would not only risk going out of business but could also drag down the reputation of the whole industry, so it has a responsibility to its rivals. Other stakeholders include the government and the communities in which firms operate.

The stakeholder approach has received a bit of a battering in recent years, not least because it was picked up enthusiastically but then soon dropped by the Labour Party under Tony Blair.

At heart, however, it seems uncontroversial. Sensible managers would always want to take into account a range of interests, both inside and outside the company. The 'good company' may even attract a better class of investors, concerned about the ethical context in which they make their money. Where the controversy arises is when corporate social responsibility is seen to overwhelm a company's main objective. Critics such as David Henderson, a former top official at the Organization for Economic Co-operation and Development, argue that the best thing firms can do for society is to make profits, which in turn generate jobs and prosperity, and that anything else is an unnecessary luxury. Managers are good at making profits, or they should be, but they are not so good at charity work. It is all a question of balance.

So far we have learned some of the fundamental economic explanations about how this restaurant, and other businesses, work, and their role in the economy. When I first studied economics I used to regard this as perhaps the least realistic part of the subject, a very long way from the cut and thrust of everyday business life. Gradually, however, I have come to see how relevant much of it is. To take an example: if you were contemplating investing in a firm you would probably want to know something about the strength of its market position, and whether it is able to deter potential competitors, so barriers to entry are important. You would probably also want to know about whether its management is focused on controlling costs and maximizing revenue, all of which comes straight out of the textbook. Economics is not business studies. But economics and business are intertwined.

⁂

The balance of this book requires that we now move on. So let us turn to another hugely influential figure, who had a rather different perspective on the role of business.

8

Mulled Marx

Our next speaker is often not thought of as an economist at all but as a political philosopher, a revolutionary and hero of many a revolution, and the subject of tens of thousands of pilgrimages to his tomb in London's Highgate cemetery. This is a strange omission, when for a time perhaps half the world was run on the principles of Marxist economics. If the late twentieth century was a victory for the economics of Adam Smith (and others), this was only after Marx had run him quite close.

Any smart restaurant might think twice about admitting Karl Marx. His spectacular beard, grey-flecked and bushy, saw him depicted in cartoons as Prometheus. To modern eyes his appearance would have been more that of a gentleman of the road. His pet name within the family was 'Moor', because of his wild appearance. In fact, the Marxist 'look' may have been based on a statue of Zeus given to him as a present, which he kept in his study. There was, however, little that was godlike about Marx, who suffered like few other mortals from carbuncles, boils (in places you would not want to know about), liver problems, insomnia, bilious attacks, migraines and respiratory complaints. A Prussian spy given the task of reporting back on Marx from Soho in London noted with disgust that 'he very seldom washes himself, combs his hair or changes his clothes' and that he enjoyed getting drunk often. Despite this, Marx fathered six children by his wife, Jenny von Westphalen, the daughter of a wealthy Prussian aristocrat, and another by the family maid, Helene 'Lenchen' Demuth. Friedrich Engels, his collaborator and benefactor, took the blame for the latter accident, claiming he was the father. Both Jenny and Lenchen are buried alongside Marx in Highgate. When Marx wrote about poverty he did so from first-hand experience. He was poor for most of his life and three of his children died in infancy. His poverty appears, however, to have been self-inflicted. He refused to take a job, even during the long periods when he suffered from writer's block, preferring to sponge off friends and benefactors, including the long-suffering Engels.

Marx was born in 1818 in Trier, Prussia (now Germany) to parents who, to avoid legal discrimination, had just converted from Judaism to Lutheranism. He studied at the University of Bonn, having already acquired a duelling scar, and came under the influence of Hegelian philosophy. By then, however, Marx was developing his own distinctive approach, which he put into practice as a journalist and then editor of the *Rheinische Zeitung*, a liberal newspaper that was too liberal for the authorities. Marx then set off with his new wife for Paris and Brussels, where he was to co-write the *Communist Manifesto* with Engels, published in 1848. (As an aside, the house in Brussels where Marx and Engels toiled came up for sale in 2002, with the estate agents hoping a wealthy Marxist would be tempted to put in an offer.) In 1849 the revolutionary thinker came to London, where he embarked on his great work, *Das Kapital*. The first volume of *Das Kapital*, or *Capital*, was published in German in 1867 and sold slowly, although an American edition, published in 1890, quickly sold its 5,000 print-run, allegedly because the publisher marketed it as a book that explained how to accumulate capital. The final two volumes of *Capital*, edited by Engels, were not published until after Marx, penniless and heartbroken following the death of his wife, himself died in 1883. Despite this, *Capital* ranks as one of the three most important economics books, along with Smith's *Wealth of Nations* and Keynes's *General Theory*.

A different kind of dismal scientist

We have seen how some of the classical economists who followed Smith took a far less optimistic view of the way capitalist economies would develop. Malthus saw population growth outstripping food supply, with disastrous consequences. Mill favoured utopian socialism to counter what modern economists would define as market failures in the distribution of income. Ricardo, while providing his famous explanation of why free trade was beneficial, also thought that landlords would be the main beneficiaries of economic growth. Workers would be trapped on subsistence wages. Marx, while borrowing the economic tools of the classical economists, including Smith, had little time for their conclusions. Malthus's grim predictions about population, he said, rested on the assumption that the capitalist system of production would continue. Under a different system there need not be a problem. The only abstract laws of population, he said, existed for 'plants and animals', not humans. Mill's utopian socialism, in the making when Marx was working on *Capital* in the reading room of the British Museum was, to Marx, both wishy-washy and wishful thinking. Marx owed his greatest economic debt to Ricardo. Both believed in the fundamental importance of distribution. If the emphasis in Smith was on the size of the economic cake, and the prospect of it growing considerably over time, Ricardo and Marx were more concerned with how it was divided. Both saw that division as leading to huge tensions. The difference was that Marx took those tensions to what he saw as their logical conclusion.

This logic, Marx's adaptation of the Hegelian 'dialectic', set him apart from other economists. His criticism of them was that they proposed laws of economics as universal and permanent as the laws of physics and chemistry, without realizing that they were describing a temporary phase in economic development. Capitalism, in Marx's view, was a mere staging post on the economic journey from feudalism to communism, its final destination. Did he have a point? While Smith has survived remarkably well through changing economic circumstances that even he could not have dreamt of, and comparative advantage is still as relevant as in Ricardo's day, it is the case, perhaps unsurprisingly, that quite a lot of the economics of the nineteenth century and before has not travelled well. Unfortunately for Marx, that is also true of most of his analysis. Before explaining why, let me sketch out some of that analysis.

The value of labour

Marx, like many of the other economists of his day, took as his starting-point the question of value. In his view the number of worker-hours needed to produce a product determined its value. If that sounds slightly odd to a modern economic observer, in an era when we know that the cost of manufacture is only a fraction of what we pay for something in the shops, it still has its echoes today. Take your car to a garage for a repair and the quote you are given will usually consist mainly of the number of hours of labour needed to do the job. Or, on a slightly grander scale, a lawyer's bill will usually be calculated on the basis of an hourly charge multiplied by the time he took for the work. Of course, nobody believes that the amount you pay to the garage goes straight into the pocket of the mechanic, or that the articled clerk who does the donkey work on your legal case gets anything like the vast sum of money you hand over to the firm. And this, essentially, was Marx's point. In any price there is value, determined by a strict interpretation of the cost of the labour required, and there is 'surplus' value, that which the owner, financier or landlord of the business obtains as a result of the sweat of the workers.

In the previous chapter I described why businesses operate on the basis of the profit motive. Without profit, potential capitalists might as well leave their money in the bank and spend their time fox hunting or on the golf course. The lure of making more money than was available in the absence of risk provided capitalists with their spur. It provided the basis for investment, without which economic development could not occur. It also gave owners of land, the landlords, incentives to allow their green fields to be turned into factory sites. Profit and rent provided the spur for development. Logical though that looks to us today, economists at the time found it hard to challenge Marx, mainly because his analysis was within a value framework that was their own. To argue that the owners of machinery deserved a return was wrong, said Marx, because the value of that machinery – defined by him as the amount of labour needed to build it – was already taken into account. As for rewards to the owners of land, this hardly came into it. In Marx's view, all property was theft.

While we can quibble with Marx's scheme, it does give us a neat way of thinking about the way he and others saw the tensions inherent in capitalism. The aim of capitalists, and in this Marx lumped owners, financiers and landlords together, was to increase surplus value. If this meant employing women and children to carry out dirty and dangerous industrial jobs, so be it. If it meant employing men to work long hours in poor conditions, that was a sound strategy. The comment of a Manchester businessman to Engels, when Marx's friend was pointing out the filth and squalor in which the working classes lived – 'And yet there is a great deal of money made here. Good morning Sir!' – seemed to sum up the attitude. Marx, though, was keen not to attach the blame to individual capitalists. They were creatures of their time, and of the system in which they operated, and their time was running out. Marx's labour theory of value provided the conflict inherent in capitalism, the battle for fair shares and the inevitability of exploitation. Marx also provided a route map to capitalism's collapse.

Capitalist crisis

On the face of it, Marx's analysis, even if it provided an accurate description of worker exploitation – all too evident at the time in the slums of Victorian England – and the abuse and ill treatment of child workers, did not necessarily explain why this process should come to an end. The capitalism described by Marx may have been a kind of industrial feudalism but why, as long as bosses could keep workers under the cosh, should it be doomed to failure? The answer, as he saw it, was that there was a dynamic process at work. Capitalists were not content to rest on their laurels, living off their profits, or 'surplus' value. Instead, they were driven by a need and by the pressures of competition from others to move things forward, by investing this surplus in yet more machinery. Marx was quite poetic about this. He wrote: 'Accumulate, accumulate! That is Moses and the prophets. Therefore save, save, i.e. reconvert the greatest possible portion of surplus value or surplus-product into capital! Accumulation for accumulation's sake, production for production's sake.'

This drive to accumulate capital, or as we would describe it, invest, had three important consequences. The first was that some workers would be displaced by machinery. In modern terminology, production changed from being labour-intensive to being capital-intensive, throwing workers in those pre-welfare state days on to the streets. This, the creation of a 'reserve army' of the unemployed was quite important in terms of worker-exploitation. As long as there were people out there willing to take a job just to eat, wages could be kept very low. The second consequence was that accumulation would result in a 'survival of the fittest', as weaker firms fell by the wayside and dominance by a few large ones became the norm. Evolution, it seemed, applied as much to capitalist economies as to the natural world. (Marx sent Charles Darwin a copy of the first volume of *Capital*, although he did not receive a response). The third and most interesting consequence, however, was that the accumulation process itself created problems for the very capitalists instituting it. Marx identified what today would be described as over-investment. Driven by the desire to accumulate and to maximize their profit, capitalists invested more than was necessary. This would drive down prices because other capitalists, with their extra investment and production, would have to compete. The process would be brutal, with small firms being driven out of business by bigger ones. It would also, in Marx's view, be part of a never-ending cycle. Capitalists, it seemed, would not learn from their mistakes. Capitalism was doomed to a declining rate of profit, which would add to the pressure on capitalists to exploit workers. It would also impose instability on the economy, as waves of accumulation – investment – were followed by retrenchment and reductions in jobs and wages.

In the Marxist scheme there were two contradictions inherent to capitalism. The first was that downtrodden workers, earning only subsistence wages, would not provide the market, the demand, for the ever-increasing amount of goods produced by the factories of the capitalists. Marx constructed an elaborate explanation of how the system could remain in balance by producing larger and larger quantities of luxury goods which the capitalists would sell to each other, but his clear implication was that this was unsustainable. Any economist would agree with him. Mass production requires mass consumption. The more fundamental contradiction lay with the workers themselves. Brought together in factories, often having moved to industrial towns and cities from the country, would they be prepared to accept their exploited plight indefinitely? Marx clearly thought not. He wrote:

> *Along with the constantly diminishing number of magnates of capital, who usurp and monopolise all advantages of this process of transformation, grows the mass of misery, oppression, slavery, degradation, exploitation; but with this too grows the revolt of the working class, a class always increasing in numbers, and disciplined, united, organised by the very mechanism of the process of capitalist production itself.*

The capitalists' own factories would become hotbeds of discontent, revolt and, ultimately, socialist revolution.

Workers of the world ...

Marx's tomb carries the slogan 'Workers of all lands unite'. That, or the more usual 'workers of the world unite', provided his rallying call. Out of Marx's *Capital* came a view of the capitalist system as not only inherently unstable and crisis-ridden but also fundamentally unfair. His labour theory of value demonstrated that capitalists were parasites on the body economic, getting fat on the surplus value created by their workers. The answer was for workers to control 'the means of production, distribution and exchange', simultaneously eliminating this surplus value (as well as the capitalists to whom it accrued) and enriching the lives of ordinary workers. Socialist parties, as well as communists, took this up. Until Tony Blair successfully abolished it soon after becoming the leader of the Labour Party in 1994, Clause Four of the party's constitution said:

> *To secure for the workers by hand or by brain the full fruits of their industry and the most equitable distribution thereof that may be possible upon the basis of the common ownership of the means of production, distribution and exchange, and the best obtainable system of popular administration and control of each industry or service.*

Exactly how far that committed Labour to Marxist state ownership was long a matter of debate. Co-operatives, for example, would appear to meet Clause Four's requirements. It was, however, used to justify the wave of nationalization by the 1945–51 Attlee government, which, as described in the previous chapter, took a whole range of industries, including coal, steel and the railways, into state ownership.

In fact, while *Capital* in its three volumes provided the theoretical justification for workers to seize the economic levers and use them, Marx and Engels had already reached this conclusion in the *Communist Manifesto* they co-wrote in 1848. While to modern eyes some of the manifesto's proposals seem revolutionary – a single monopoly state bank, monopoly state ownership of transport and communication and the abolition of property rights – others are quite mild. It proposed a graduated or progressive income tax and the extension of state ownership of factories and other means of production, but not complete control.

How wrong was Marx?

Marx was one of the most influential thinkers of the modern era, but history has not been kind to his economics. The rise of the middle classes in western capitalist societies defied his prediction of workers kept permanently in conditions of near-poverty. Capitalism has been kinder to the masses than communism. There were crises of capitalism, most notably in the Great Depression of the 1930s, and there was of course the Russian revolution of 1917. But Marx's central prediction, of capitalist crises brought on by falling profits, did not stand the test of time. The domino-like fall of communism in Eastern Europe at the end of the 1980s, most dramatically with the collapse of the Berlin Wall, and its present minority status, pursued by only a few oddball countries, appears to signal that little more than a century after his death, Marx's star has waned, possibly never to resurge. The record of economies run along Marxist lines, ostensibly for the benefit of the workers, was abysmal. Before the unification of West and East Germany in 1990, there was a widespread impression that the economy in the east, the old German Democratic Republic, was quite strong. Only when it was opened up to full view were its weaknesses revealed. Marx's economics has not lasted. Keynes set the tone in the 1930s by describing *Capital* as 'scientifically erroneous' and 'without interest or application in the modern world'. Marxist thought, he said, was based on a misunderstanding of Ricardo's theory of value. That was a little harsh, owing much to the benefit of hindsight. The classical economists were seriously challenged by Marx's critique and, in its time, his work provided an intellectual underpinning to the revolutionaries threatening the capitalism of the industrial age. The capitalists of the period and their intellectual supporters would have given short shrift to the suggestion that Marx did not represent a threat.

That is partly why his predictions were wrong. Even if you were to accept an analysis that suggested workers would tend to remain permanently downtrodden, this did not leave revolution as the only solution. Worker power could be and was exerted through other ways, not least through democratic socialist parties. A Marxist analysis would say that capitalism adapted, steering a course that accepted, under pressure, a more equitable distribution of income. Adam Smith would have said that this was always the way it was going to be.

Defenders of Marx, responding to the fact that workers had indeed made economic progress, enjoying rising living standards rather than stagnating on the breadline, used to point to the exploitation by industrial countries of their colonies. In other words, western workers had prospered only because of the downtrodden poor elsewhere. There is a flavour of that in the present debate over globalization. When the richest 200 people in the world have the combined income of the poorest 41 per cent of the global population, or nearly half of the people of the world live on less than $2 a day, the existence of inequality is not in doubt. What is harder, however, is to argue that this emerges from Marx's scheme of things. Inequality arises as much from the inability of so many people to participate in the capitalist process, for reasons I shall come on to later. The links between global inequality and Marx's economics are at best tenuous, at worst do not exist at all.

9

Paying the bill

Now that Marx has left us, muttering ever so slightly and with a bottle of capitalist champagne concealed under his coat, it is time to start thinking about something that can ruin any meal – paying the bill. We are not quite at the end of our meal yet, and some might say this is a contrived title for a chapter about what governments do. But it seems fair enough to me. The government's most important role in the economy is, after all, raising taxation, for which we all have to pick up the bill, and redistributing it in the form of public expenditure. Sir Leo Pliatsky, a former senior civil servant at the Treasury and Department of Trade and Industry, called his memoirs *Getting and Spending*, after Wordsworth's 'getting and spending we lay waste our powers'. So let us have a look at the government's core role in the economy, at fiscal policy. Fiscal means 'pertaining to tax' but fiscal policy is both government spending and taxation.

Why governments spend

These days the fact that governments spend many billions each year is taken for granted. As long as there have been governments there has been government spending. It is worth thinking briefly about why this is. The first justification comes with so-called 'public goods'. These are services or institutions that benefit the community as a whole but which the public would be unlikely to pay for on a voluntary basis. Would we pay voluntarily for the police service? Perhaps not if we believed the headlines that say they spend all their time persecuting middle-class motorists rather than catching criminals. Would we fund the legal system, which is necessary but expensive, with all those highly paid lawyers and judges? And, while there is no shortage of patriotism at time of war, citizens might object to the cost of maintaining the armed forces when there is no threat on the horizon. The existence of public goods is one type of 'market failure'. If the government did not provide them, they probably would not exist and a properly functioning legal system, for example, is necessary to the workings of the economy.

A second type of market failure comes with so-called uninsurable risks. Would a chronically sick person with no income be able to get private health insurance? No, unless the government required insurance companies to provide blanket coverage for everybody within an area. Even then, to spread the risks between the healthy and unhealthy, companies might be required to offer such cover across a very wide area. And if this is the case why should not the government itself offer or at least guarantee such insurance, paid for out of taxation? The same goes for a whole range of risks, including unemployment insurance for the persistently unemployed and sickness pay for regular absentees. Even if the government acts as insurer, or purchaser, it does not have to be provider as well. The government could buy its entire healthcare on behalf of patients from private sector doctors and hospitals, removing the need for a National Health Service. At time of writing it is doing that but only at the margin. The argument for an NHS funded out of taxation was that only a large organization (the biggest employer in Western Europe) could take advantage of economies of scale, provide healthcare even in sparsely populated areas and train sufficient staff.

While most economists accept that it is the role of government to provide public goods, its role in the areas of uninsurable risks and as a provider of services such as health and education has come to be challenged, although not yet by enough people to change the system significantly, at least in Britain. Similarly, governments use taxation and government spending to redistribute income from rich to poor. Free market economists would argue that modern governments have moved well beyond what should be their core competences. There is little prospect, however, of a return to smaller, simpler government.

Spend, and spend some more
Budgetary arrangements differ between countries, notably in the split between central and local, or federal and state, when it comes both to revenue-raising and spending. The basic rules are, however, the same everywhere. Revenues are raised to finance

spending. If more revenues are raised than needed there is a budget surplus. If revenues are insufficient there is a budget deficit and the government – central, local, federal or state – has to borrow to make up the difference. That, in a paragraph, is public finance.

UK government spending, at the time of writing, is about £400 billion a year, in an economy with a GDP of some £1,000 billion, so roughly 40 per cent. Under current arrangements, the level of spending is negotiated between the Treasury and other Whitehall departments on a three-year rolling basis. A Comprehensive Spending Review (CSR) occurs every two years, the third year of each settlement being the first year of the next. A significant portion of this spending is in the form of transfer payments – pensions and welfare benefits – and so should not be double-counted for GDP purposes. Even so, that 40 per cent figure is fair to take when analysing the growth in public spending. The other main distinction is between current and capital expenditure. In the National Health Service, for example, current expenditure would include wages and salaries of doctors, nurses and other staff, and the annual drugs bill, while building a new hospital would plainly count as capital expenditure. The lion's share of government spending is current. In recent years public–private partnerships, such as the private finance initiative (PFI), have been used to try to increase the amount of capital spending.

Before the twentieth century, the story of public spending was essentially one of war and peace. Governments spent, by and large, to maintain armies, and that spending rose sharply during times of war, when those armies swelled in numbers. Before the Napoleonic wars, for example, the British government spent about a tenth of GDP, a figure that rose to a third by the time of the Battle of Waterloo. Wars were expensive, and still are, necessitating both higher taxation and, more importantly, extensive and prolonged borrowing. That was not just a pre-twentieth century phenomenon. The burden of financing the Second World War seriously sapped Britain's ability to continue as a major economic power in the post-war period.

Until 1914 public expenditure operated around a peacetime norm of 10 or 11 per cent of GDP. This was the level in the early part of the century, the late Victorian and Edwardian eras. The First World War effectively ushered in a period of state control of the economy and, in its aftermath, public spending did not return to its peacetime norm, instead settling at a little over 20 per cent of GDP. This was not just due to the cost of paying for the war, in terms of the interest on government debt, but also because of the beginnings of a government-provided welfare state. The Liberal government elected in 1906 passed legislation in 1908 introducing state old-age pensions, as well as David Lloyd George's 1911 National Insurance Act, which provided elements of both unemployment and health insurance. This ratcheting higher of spending continued during and after the Second World War, a period that saw the Education Act of 1944, the National Health Service Act of 1946 (the NHS came into being in 1948), the National Insurance Act of 1946 and the National Assistance Act of 1948. This was the period when, following Sir William Beveridge's 1942 report, the modern welfare state came into being, with the government taking responsibility for health, education, pensions and a range of benefits covering unemployment, sickness and other needs. It was also a time when state control of industry was significantly extended. By the early 1950s government spending had reached 30 to 35 per cent of GDP, increasing further to between 45 and 50 per cent by the mid-1970s, as welfare spending rose. The Thatcher government succeeded in reducing it, on average, to about 40 per cent of GDP, where it has stayed.

The rise of government spending to about four times its pre-1914 level relative to the size of the economy, has been accompanied by significant changes in its composition. As recently as 1950, defence was the most important item of government spending, equivalent to 6.6 per cent of GDP, followed by social security (5.1 per cent), health (3.6 per cent), education (3.4 per cent) and housing (2.6 per cent). Half a century later, social security had the biggest budget (12.4 per cent of GDP), followed by health and personal social services (6.7 per cent), education (4.6 per cent) and defence (2.7 per cent). The rise of the welfare state is clear, as is the declining importance of defence, the more so since the British government, like others, claimed the 'peace dividend' following the end of the Cold War. Housing, important in the period following both world wars – building 'homes fit for heroes' – has turned into only a tiny part of government spending, following the Thatcher government's successful policy of selling council houses to their tenants, and the transfer of much of the remaining council housing stock to housing associations.

What is the right level of government spending?

How come it used to be the case that governments spent only a tenth of GDP on public services, and much of that on defence, whereas two-fifths is now regarded as the norm? Part of the reason is that in the past there was no universal state provision of education, healthcare and support for the poor. This did not mean there was no such provision. In Britain a network of voluntary organizations, charities, medical aid societies, friendly societies and churches, often acting with local or national government agencies, provided an informal welfare state long before Beveridge. School boards ensured most local children received an education well before the 1944 Education Act. One criticism of the post-war welfare state was that it swept aside many of these highly effective voluntary arrangements. Paying to see a doctor was commonplace, indeed expected. Many operated an informal system of cross-subsidies, making sure their wealthier patients paid but not chasing up the fees of poorer clients. On the first day of the NHS, 5 July 1948, many patients turned up at GP surgeries armed with their sixpences, it not having sunk in that from then on consultations and treatments would be 'free at the point of delivery'. They soon became used to it. Within a few months the cost of the NHS was rising at a rate that alarmed ministers, a pattern that has continued to this day. Aneurin Bevan, the 'father of the NHS' in the post-1945 Labour government, was soon commenting: 'I shudder to think of the ceaseless cascade of medicine which is pouring down British throats at the present time.'

The level of public spending varies over time and it also varies in content. Britain's defence budget relative to the size of the economy has steadily shrunk with the dismantling of the Empire. Housing is no longer a priority area for government spending. When the Conservatives were in power from 1979 to 1997, some areas of the welfare state were chipped away and replaced by private insurance, for example indefinitely paying the mortgage payments of the unemployed. A policy was also put in place to reduce the attractiveness of the basic state old-age pension, and by implication increasing the incentive to contribute to private arrangements, by linking annual rises in the state pension to prices rather than faster-growing earnings. Privatization dramatically reduced the state's role in the UK economy during the 1980s and early 1990s, transferring telecommunications, steel, gas, water and electricity from public to private sectors, whereas the earlier policy of nationalization had increased it.

The point is that there is no economically determined optimum for the level of government spending. It is a matter of political choice. It is also a matter of national preference. Britain's 40 per cent of GDP level (39.4 per cent in 2002 according to the OECD) is high in relation to the United States, where around 30 per cent (31.2 per cent in 2002) is the norm. But it is low in comparison with other EU countries such as Germany, 46.2 per cent, France, 50.9 per cent, or Sweden, 53 per cent. The fact that the level of spending is a political choice does not mean, of course, that it has no economic effects.

Getting crowded

'There's no such thing as a free lunch' is the motto for this book, and there is no such thing as costless government spending. When Bevan fretted about the embryonic NHS's medicine bill, it was because the market mechanism had been removed. For the first time there was no price constraint – the cost of a visit to the GP or of the medicine itself – on people's healthcare. This is why, when services are funded out of taxation, rationing is common and, indeed, has been a feature of the NHS since its creation. The benefits of government spending are many. Governments can, through taxation, put money to more socially desirable uses. They can spend to keep the economy going during hard times (more of that shortly) or to help out hard-hit regions. However, there are costs too, and one way of thinking about these is in terms of crowding out.

What is crowding out? Right at the very start of this book I picked up on one of the commonly used definitions of economics, the one about it being all about the allocation of scarce resources. That definition is quite useful in the context of government spending, in two respects. The first is that markets achieve that allocation by means of price. Products that are in short supply will rise in price, restricting the demand for them, and encouraging people to switch to things that are cheaper and more plentiful. 'Free' public services such as healthcare operate in the absence of any price mechanism. Demand, as a result, can be limitless. This is why rationing is so common in public healthcare and other services. The second way the allocation of resources comes in useful as a concept is in thinking about the way the economy divides up between public and private sectors.

A computer expert employed full-time by the Inland Revenue cannot also be employed by the private sector. The office in which he works cannot also be used for commercial purposes. A pound taken in tax and used to fund the NHS cannot also be spent by the individual for half a pint of beer. It has gone. The government, in carrying out public services, stakes a claim on a substantial slice of the economy's resources, whether they are people, property, equipment, or the money to pay for all these things. 'Resource' crowding out occurs when the government's claims on these things act to the detriment of the private sector. When might this arise? Suppose there is a limited number of IT experts and the private sector cannot get hold of trained staff because the government is employing most of them. Or Whitehall departments take all the best office locations in the centre of London. More generally, resource crowding out arises when resources are fully used. If the economy is in a situation of full employment, for example, the private sector will be unable to take on extra staff unless it is able to recruit them from the public sector. If the public sector does not want to let them go, or is recruiting too, the effect will be to push up wages, and therefore both private and public sector costs.

There is another type of crowding out. What happens when governments increase spending at a faster rate than tax revenues are flowing in? Governments are required to borrow, to run a budget deficit. All governments borrow, usually from their own citizens and financial institutions, in the form of National Savings or the issue of government bonds (called gilts in the UK because the certificates originally had gold edging). Borrowing by governments is perfectly normal. The problem arises when governments try to borrow too much. Originally people used to think about financial crowding out in the sense that, if there was a limited supply of funds, the more the government claimed for its own purposes the less would be available for companies to raise in order to finance productive investment. In these days of global, free-flowing capital between different countries, it is wrong to think of a narrowly defined pool of money existing only in one country. International investors buy the bonds issued by the governments of other countries. Japanese financial institutions, famously, allowed America to run big budget deficits from the mid-1980s onwards by their willingness to buy US government bonds, so-called treasuries. These days a more subtle form of crowding out can occur. Governments that borrow heavily will be regarded with some suspicion by the financial markets, which will require a higher rate of interest in return for providing funds. The effect of heavy government borrowing is to push up interest rates for all borrowers, which has the effect of crowding out some of them. This is one reason why the euro operates under a 'Stability and Growth' Pact, under which member governments are required to restrict their budget deficits to 3 per cent of GDP or below. The fear behind it was that heavy borrowing by one member country could have a damaging effect throughout the euro area.

Multiplying government spending

Before moving on to tax, and the 'Budget judgment', one quick point. Our next speaker, John Maynard Keynes, will have a little more to say on this, but it is necessary to qualify very slightly the effect of government spending. A pound spent by the government cannot be used by you or me to buy books or groceries but some of that pound may indeed end up being spent on such things. How so? Approximately 70 per cent of health service spending goes on wages and salaries. It therefore provides public sector employees with an income, part of which they will use for, yes, books and groceries. Some of the non-wage component of public spending will be used to pay for supplies or services that, again, will provide somebody with an income. An initial increase in government spending flows around the economy for quite a while. Just like with a pebble tossed into a pool, the effects go beyond the initial splash. A pound spent by the government does not, however, produce a pound of spending at the next stage. Some of the income paid out by the health service will be taken by tax, some will be spent on imports, some saved. But the multiplier is a useful idea. Sometimes it is used to justify extra government spending rather than tax cuts, on the ground that cutting taxes for individuals will be subject to quite large leakages because, for example, three-quarters of cars sold in Britain are imported. Government spending, as Americans used to say (some still do), carries 'more bang for the buck'.

Taxing time – the Budget

Budget day, held in March or April, is one of the great occasions in the British political calendar, and the big date in the UK economic calendar. Many other countries have a single day each year when the finance minister makes his annual Budget statement. In the United States, where the Budget is the product of long and often messy negotiation between the White House and Congress, the process is less clear-cut. Again, though, the principles are similar the world over.

In the UK the days may have gone when MPs would queue for hours to be sure of securing their place in the House of Commons chamber for the Chancellor's speech, but 3.30 on Budget afternoon, when the speech is delivered, is still guaranteed to be one of the few times when it is full to overflowing. The term 'budget' derives from the French '*bougette*', a wallet or pouch, of the kind Robert Walpole used to carry his papers in when he was Chancellor in the 1730s. Nowadays Chancellors carry a more familiar red Budget dispatch box, holding it aloft for photographers outside 11 Downing Street before making the short journey to the Palace of Westminster. Today, too, Chancellors read prepared texts, in the knowledge that a stray word could be misinterpreted in the financial markets. It was not always like this. William Gladstone's legendary four-hour speeches were made from brief notes, one set of which is on display in the Museum of London. The Budget is preceded by weeks of speculation, some of it informed, some of it leaked, deliberately or otherwise. Only one Chancellor, Hugh Dalton, has resigned for leaking the Budget. In 1947 he inadvertently let slip some of its contents to a reporter from a London evening paper, who was able to get it into the paper and on the streets before Dalton had made his speech to the House of Commons. In 1984 a disgruntled civil servant leaked the entire contents of the Budget to the *Guardian*. A police investigation was launched, but the culprit was never caught. Why the obsession with secrecy? Because some Budget information is market-sensitive and because foreknowledge can allow people to take action. The 1984 leak was important not only because the Budget contained some important changes to corporate taxation, but also because it included, from midnight on the day of the speech, the removal of tax relief on life insurance policies. The leak produced a two-week rush to take out such insurance, and thus to continue to benefit from the tax break, and cost the government tens of millions in lost revenue.

A Budget speech usually consists of a review of the economy's prospects, including a new forecast from the Treasury (it is required by law, the 1975 Industry Act, to produce two a year). The Chancellor will also run through the state of the public finances and whether the government plans to borrow, in other words run a budget deficit, or repay debt, which would mean a budget surplus. There will also probably be some public spending announcements although since 1998 the main occasion for announcing these has been in the Comprehensive Spending Review (CSR), which concludes in the summer and is held every two years. From 1993 to 1996 the Conservative government broke with tradition and held a 'unified' Budget, with both spending and tax announcements, in the autumn. Labour, on taking office in 1997 reverted to spring Budgets. And the main purpose of the spring Budget, as it has been for centuries, is to raise tax.

Taxes and the Budget judgment

In the 2001–2 tax year UK government receipts totalled about
£395 billion, a considerable sum. Income tax, introduced 200
years ago by William Pitt the Younger, is easily the most important single tax, bringing in £108 billion. It was followed by
National Insurance contributions, at £65 billion. NI contributions, paid by both employers and employees (and the self-
employed) are an example of direct taxation. They are levied
according to income, as of course is income tax, and have to be
paid. Indirect taxation, in contrast, can be avoided, usually by
the act of not purchasing the goods on which it is levied. If you
do not smoke, drink or drive, you will escape the duties and
value-added tax (VAT) levied on these activities. VAT, which
brought in £61 billion in 2001–2, is the third biggest tax. It is
harder to avoid but not impossible. Food, books, newspapers
and children's clothing and footwear are all zero-rated for VAT
purposes. A small person whose only hobby was reading would
pay very little VAT. The fourth biggest tax, another direct tax,
is corporation tax, levied on the income of companies. It
brought in £34 billion. These four taxes together accounted for
the lion's share of the government's income, £268 billion, or
more than two-thirds of the total. Other significant taxes were
fuel duties, £22 billion; duties on alcohol and tobacco, £14.5
billion; business rates, £17.5 billion; and council tax, £15 billion.

The 'Budget judgment' is, at its simplest, the net amount the
Chancellor intends to raise or lower taxation in the coming year.
In practice it can get a little more complicated, because Chan-

cellors often announce deferred tax changes that will take effect
only in future years. The principle is, however, the same. I shall
come to what determines that judgment but first a small note of
clarification. On the face of it, some taxes always go up in a
Budget. Smokers, drinkers and motorists have become used to
the idea that duties, and therefore prices, rise after the Budget.
But some taxes also usually go down. Most income taxpayers
will find, a month or so after the Budget, a small reduction in the
amount of tax they pay. There is, fortunately, an easy explanation for this, and it has nothing to do with the Budget judgment.
It is conventional for income tax allowances to be lifted each
year in line with inflation – to be 'indexed' (increased by the rise
in the retail prices index). A parliamentary amendment – the
Rooker–Wise amendment – introduced during the high inflation of the 1970s, requires Chancellors to do this unless they
have got good reason not to. Hence the appearance of an
income tax cut – in fact just handing back the extra tax you are
paying because of inflation – each year. Chancellors have a way
of getting this money back, mainly by indexing petrol, tobacco
and alcohol duties. This is why the prices of these tend to rise
after Budgets. It is also why these 'indexation' effects, which are
more or less automatic, should be put aside when we are trying
to assess whether taxes are being raised or lowered.

On this basis a typical Budget 'giveaway', an expansionary
Budget, involves between £2 billion and £3 billion of tax cuts,
while a tough Budget might raise them by a similar amount.
This is small in relation to government receipts – 0.5 to 0.75 per
cent – and even smaller in relation to the size of the economy,

0.2 to 0.3 per cent. Some Budgets do go further. In 1988 Nigel Lawson cut the top rate of income tax from 60 to 40 per cent and the basic rate from 27 to 25 per cent. That giveaway was worth, at year 2000 prices, £7–8 billion. A few years earlier, in 1981, his Conservative predecessor Sir Geoffrey Howe had raised taxes by a similar amount. Gordon Brown, in his April 2002 Budget, also increased taxes by £7–8 billion a year, mostly through higher National Insurance contributions for both employers and employees, mainly to fund extra National Health Service spending.

From fine-tuning to no tuning

If the amounts involved in Budget tax changes are generally small in relation to the size of the economy, so too are the ambitions of politicians. From the early 1950s onwards, under the influence of the followers of Keynes – he will be with us in a minute – 'fine-tuning' was in vogue. The economy was subject to well-observed cyclical fluctuations, lasting about four years. For a year or two things would be slack then they would pick up, gaining momentum until the point when a boom was under way. These cyclical fluctuations were due to variations in demand, so what better than to try and iron them out by small changes in tax? In a downturn, putting more money into the hands of consumers and businesses by lowering taxes would stimulate spending, thereby lessening the severity of that downswing in activity. Politicians of the day, such as Harold Macmillan, who was both Chancellor and Prime Minister (though not at the same time), used to talk of 'a dab on the accelerator'. In an upturn, when the need was for consumers and businesses to cool their spending ardour, taxes would be raised slightly, 'a touch on the brake'. Why? Because otherwise the economy would carry on growing faster than its long-run rate, unemployment would fall to very low levels and the pressures on capacity would push up inflation. There was even a formal mechanism for fine-tuning, the 'regulator' introduced in the early 1960s, which allowed the Chancellor to vary most indirect taxes – purchase tax (VAT's predecessor) and the excise duties on tobacco, alcohol and petrol – by 10 per cent in either direction between budgets.

Today, although politicians often talk about tax changes as being timely, fine-tuning through tax is no more. It was killed off by the realization that it was inefficient – tax changes, particularly direct ones, can usually be introduced only slowly and then take time to feed through to pay packets. This is partly because budgets are infrequent, usually only once a year (emergency budgets smack of panic), and take time to pass through the parliamentary process. A tax cut introduced during a downturn may actually have its impact in the subsequent boom, when the opposite is required. Fiscal fine-tuning was also killed off by the boom-and-bust cycles of the 1970s and 1980s. These needed, if it were available, not so much fine-tuning as a major overhaul.

Fiscal rules

In place of fine-tuning, governments now tend to operate on the basis of so-called fiscal rules. In the case of the countries that have adopted the European single currency, the euro, the rules come under the so-called Stability and Growth Pact. This requires that countries usually run a balanced budget – with spending and taxation roughly equal – and should not allow deficits to exceed 3 per cent of GDP in other circumstances. The Labour government elected in 1997 adopted two such rules. The first was the 'golden' rule, that over the economic cycle it would borrow only to invest – build new hospitals, schools and roads – and not to finance current spending on, for example, the wages and salaries of public sector workers. The second was what it called the sustainable investment rule, which was to hold government debt, the national debt, at a 'stable and prudent' level – in practice below 40 per cent of GDP. The national debt, which dates back to the Napoleonic wars and before, is currently around £300 billion, or 30 per cent of GDP. Governments have reduced it but never quite succeeded in paying it off. Britain's debt is low by international standards. The Maastricht criteria for countries joining the euro required that they reduce their debt to less than 60 per cent of GDP.

Fiscal rules are in fashion and nowadays any fine-tuning occurs through interest rate changes, through monetary policy. The purpose of taxation is rather different. What is it?

Taxes and behaviour

At its most basic the purpose of taxation is to raise the money governments need to finance their spending. The effects of taxation, however, go well beyond that. Adam Smith gave us the four 'canons' of taxation: that it should be based on ability to pay; that it should be 'certain' – taxpayers should know how much they have to pay and when; that it should be convenient to pay; and that taxes should be relatively cheap to collect – relative to the amount of revenue they raise, they should be 'economical'. Ability to pay is perhaps the one that features most prominently in modern tax debates. 'Progressive' income tax regimes – where higher earners pay higher marginal rates (the rate of tax on the last pound of income) and therefore a greater proportion of their earnings in tax – exist in the majority of countries. In Britain there is a starting rate of income tax of 10 per cent and a top rate of 40 per cent. Such regimes have faced a challenge, however, from mainly right-wing advocates of a flat-rate income tax, in which the amount paid would simply rise in line with income. Under a flat tax of, say 30 per cent, the £100,000 earner would pay the same marginal rate as a £20,000 earner but would also, because of higher earnings, face a bigger tax bill. The ability to pay principle would be satisfied, although not to the same extent as with a progressive tax.

All taxes distort. Many people will have seen some of the windows of otherwise pristine old houses in Britain bricked up, a legacy of the infamous window tax, introduced in 1696 and abolished in 1851, under which properties with ten or more windows were subject to additional taxation. More recently the poll tax or community charge, brought in as a form of local government taxation in 1990 (and widely seen as a factor behind Margaret Thatcher's downfall), led many young people to remove themselves from the electoral register, thus depriving themselves of the opportunity of voting, rather than pay the tax.

The precise way in which income tax distorts will depend on

circumstances – an increase in income tax rates could either make people work more to maintain their previous post-tax income, or work less because the incentive to earn more has been reduced. Taxes on employment, such as the National Insurance contributions employers have to pay, will, by raising the cost of each worker, tend to reduce numbers employed. The high social security costs – the equivalent of NI – faced by employers in much of Europe are one reason for lower levels of employment, and higher unemployment, there. Indirect taxes such as VAT or excise duties on alcohol, tobacco and petrol will, other things being equal, have the effect of reducing the consumption of such products by raising their price. This was recognized in the principle of the regulator, described above. The extent to which changes in such taxes increase or reduce consumption will depend both on what is happening to income and whether demand for the product is 'elastic' (highly responsive to price changes) or inelastic. Indexation, merely increasing duties in line with inflation, is unlikely to have much impact on consumption. Indeed, if earnings are rising faster than prices, as is usually the case, the effects of indexation will be to make the product cheaper in relation to income. Say earnings are rising at 5 per cent a year and inflation is 2.5 per cent. Increasing duties by 2.5 per cent would still leave them cheaper relatively to earnings. They need to rise by at least 5 per cent. This is one reason why duties on goods regarded as bad for health or the environment – tobacco, alcohol, petrol – are often 'over-indexed', raised by more than the inflation rate. The trouble with this is that, thanks to the EU Single Market and some well-organized smuggling operations, UK consumers of tobacco and alcohol have access to cheaper supplies. Smuggling costs the Treasury billions each year in lost revenues. Legal and illegal imports of such products may mean that the unintended consequence of raising duties for health reasons is that increasing numbers of consumers have access to them at lower prices than before.

VAT, 17.5 per cent at the time of writing, is not formally indexed but the revenue from it will tend to rise in line with the level of spending, reflecting both inflation and changes in the volume of purchases.

Laffer and the 'right' level of tax

Under Margaret Thatcher in Britain and Ronald Reagan in America, the supply-side revolution of the 1980s, there was a deliberate rejection of the idea that taxation should be used for fine-tuning purposes. An important part of that revolution was a powerful belief that high taxation in general, and high taxes on income in particular, distorts. Tax the rewards of success too heavily, it was argued, and people will have no incentive to take the risks necessary to achieve success. High tax rates on company directors will stifle enterprise. Ability to pay, in other words, can go only so far before it starts to do some damage. Moreover, if tax rates are set too high, their effect will be to *reduce* the amount of revenue the government receives.

In the late 1970s Arthur Laffer, an economics professor who held positions at the universities of both Chicago and Southern California, was having lunch in a Washington restaurant with Jude Wanniski of the *Wall Street Journal*. Laffer sketched out on a napkin the way in which high tax rates could cut revenue. If the income tax rate is zero, then the government gets no revenue. But if it is 100 per cent, the government is also penniless, because there is no point anybody working for a zero post-tax income. Between those two points, Laffer demonstrated, there will be a rate of tax above which revenue starts to decline. Initially, say from zero to 50 per cent, higher rates swell government revenues. Somewhere around that point, however, the opposite will occur and the government will find itself, having raised tax, worse off. The Laffer curve, which is usually dome-shaped, with the optimum tax rate somewhere in the middle (although Thatcher, Reagan and the supply-siders would always think of anything like a 50 per cent income tax rate, even as the top marginal rate, as too high).

The idea that raising tax can reduce revenue is not confined to direct taxes and their disincentive effects. When, under the European Single Market, the rules governing personal imports of cigarettes, wine, spirits and beer into Britain from the rest of the EU were relaxed, the tobacco and drinks lobby argued, with some conviction, that increasing taxes on these items in Britain was having precisely this effect. The more the British government taxed, the more the incentive for individuals, as well as organized gangs of smugglers, to exploit the 'Calais run'. By the year 2001 the Treasury was losing £3 billion a year in tobacco taxes alone.

Earmarking or stealth?
When the Labour government took office in 1997, it immedi-

ately set about raising taxes. Mostly it did this in a subtle, or 'stealthy', way. It fulfilled an election promise by imposing a £5 billion one-off, or windfall, tax on the former nationalized industries such as gas, electricity and water that, it said, had made excessive (monopoly) profits in the private sector. It also announced a change that would be worth £5 billion a year by abolishing a tax credit on company dividends previously enjoyed by pension funds. This was a stealthy change because most individuals would not become aware of it until retirement, by which time it would have been wrapped up in a series of other factors affecting long-term pension fund performance. Stealth taxes can, however, backfire. One of the others the government used was to take advantage of weak world oil prices to sharply increase the duty on petrol. Because falling world prices were compensating for rising tax, nobody noticed. But in September 2000, when the world oil price surged higher, petrol prices also increased and the government, not the Organization of Petroleum Exporting Countries, got the blame. In a humiliating climb-down the Chancellor, Gordon Brown, was forced to cut the duties.

The opposite of a stealth tax is one that is raised for a specific purpose – an earmarked or 'hypothecated' tax. In November 2001 the government published an independent report, the Wanless report, which said that the National Health Service needed substantial additional resources. This sparked a debate about introducing a hypothecated health tax. The Treasury rejected it, saying it would be wrong to link health spending to the revenue from a tax that could vary from year to year. Instead it raised National Insurance in the Budget a few months later.

The Treasury's real reason for caution about hypothecation, which is a long-standing objection, is that while people might be prepared to pay a health tax, they might object to a tax that had as its purpose raising the money to pay out welfare benefits. Even defence, a traditional public good, might struggle to raise money if it were given its own hypothecated tax.

Taxes, credits and reliefs

In the past two or three decades there has been a tendency in most countries to move from direct to indirect taxes, for supply-side, or incentive reasons – the idea being that if people keep more of what they earn they will work harder. Even so, direct taxes are still more important in terms of raising revenue. The top marginal rate of income tax in Britain was reduced from 83 to 40 per cent between 1979 and 1988, while the main rate of VAT increased from 8 per cent in 1979 to 17.5 per cent in 1991.

Another favoured shift has been to achieve lower tax rates by limiting tax reliefs. A tax relief is an amount that can be set against the amount of tax an individual or company pays. Every taxpayer in Britain has a personal allowance – £4,535 in 2001–2 – the amount that can be earned before any tax is paid. Until relatively recently, most households also benefited from tax relief on their mortgages. For borrowings of up to £30,000, mortgage interest attracted tax relief. At times of high interest rates this implied a hefty bill – in terms of lost taxation – for the Treasury. The relief was pared down before being abolished entirely by the Blair government. So too was the married couple's allowance, effectively an additional tax relief received by married men. The writing had been on the wall for that relief since the introduction in the 1980s of separate taxation for husbands and wives.

While tax reliefs have been scaled back, tax credits have come into vogue. What is a tax credit? For a long time the holy grail of tax reformers was a negative income tax. The idea was a smooth transition from low earners, who not only did not pay tax but also received money back from the tax authorities, to higher earners who paid tax. Tax credits work a little like that. The working families' tax credit, introduced in Britain by the 1997 Labour government, directly replaced a welfare benefit (family credit), the difference being that low earners received a top-up not from the social security office but from their employer in their pay packet (the money being subsequently refunded by the Inland Revenue). The working families' tax credit, due to be renamed the working tax credit in 2003–4, will operate alongside a child credit – payments through the tax system for lower- and middle-income families.

*
**

That's probably enough about tax and public spending. As always, there is no shortage of information on this subject, nor limits to the scope for change. Chancellors have a Budget once a year and usually find a way of tinkering with the system, often by introducing new taxes. The best independent guide through the tax and spending maze is the Institute for Fiscal Studies (www.ifs.org.uk). Its annual Green Budget, published a little in advance of the actual Budget, is an invaluable aid. The site also contains useful information on comparative tax systems.

And now – I have been hinting at his arrival for some time – the moment has come. Given that Adam Smith was Scottish, our next guest must rank as the greatest English economist, although David Ricardo has his fair share of supporters. Anyway, there can be no doubt that John Maynard Keynes was the greatest modern British economist, and one of the towering figures of the twentieth century.

10

Keynes gets cooking

If the title of this chapter makes Keynes sound like a master chef, showy magician might be more appropriate. Keynes weaved his spell over economics at a time when the subject was growing into a mainstream area of study in universities. *Time* magazine named him the greatest economist of the twentieth century and, in truth, there were no other serious candidates to challenge him. For the past seventy to eighty years the economic debate has been dominated by Keynes, both by those who followed and developed his ideas and, as importantly, by those who sought to challenge them. When, after the 11 September 2001 terrorist attacks on America, the Bush administration pushed a programme of tax cuts and additional government spending to head off recession, it was, said commentators, because Washington had rediscovered Keynes. That was not quite right. Keynes had never really gone away.

Who was he? John Maynard Keynes, always known as Maynard to friends and colleagues, was born in 1883, the year of
Marx's lonely death. His father, John Neville Keynes, was a distinguished economics professor at Cambridge, although not as
distinguished as Alfred Marshall, his contemporary. Marshall,
who later taught the younger Keynes, is worth a brief digression.
When we left English classical economics it was in a state of
some disarray, Marx having emerged to challenge some of its
cosy, and not-so-cosy, assumptions. Marshall's great contribution was to put classical economics into a coherent framework,
recognizable to economics students today. His *Principles of Economics*, published in 1890, not only provided the first clear signal
that economics was to develop as a science, rather than as the art
of political economy, but it demonstrated how the 'marginals' –
marginal cost, marginal revenue and marginal utility – that we
have already encountered, fitted in. If Smith, Ricardo, Mill et al.
were classical economists, Marshall's approach was 'neo-classi-
cal', adapting and setting their work in what was then a modern
context. Keynes is sometimes said to have thrown his teacher's
work back in his face by overturning some of its assumptions,
but that is not really fair. Marshall was concerned mainly with
microeconomics, the working of individual markets, Keynes's
main area of influence was macroeconomics.

After studying at Eton Keynes returned to Cambridge to read
not economics but mathematics, in which he took a degree.
While there he became an Apostle, a member of the university's
elite secret society, and also – perhaps because of that society's
belief in the superiority of homosexual love, perhaps because of

his time at Eton – a practising homosexual. He did, however, apparently renounce homosexuality on his unlikely marriage in 1925 to the Russian ballerina Lydia Lopokova, who was to prove a great source of support during his later life, particularly after his first heart attack in 1937. Keynes entered the India Office (part of what is now the Foreign Office) in 1909, staying only two years before returning to Cambridge as a teaching fellow in economics, his skills in the subject having been both noticed and encouraged by Marshall. Almost immediately he became editor of the prestigious *Economic Journal*.

The First World War and its aftermath were to be the making of Keynes, as we shall see, but even a brief account of his life could not leave out his extraordinary renaissance man qualities. He was a member of the Bloomsbury group, which included Virginia Woolf and Lytton Strachey, and Keynes's own writing was much admired for its elegance. Indeed, some of his best sayings rival Oscar Wilde's. 'I would rather be vaguely right, than precisely wrong,' he said, and: 'I do not know which makes a man more conservative – to know nothing but the present, or nothing but the past.' He could also be wonderfully cutting. Of one senior Treasury mandarin, he wrote that 'he could stay silent in several languages'. Of another that 'caught young', he might have understood the elements of economics. He often attracted wit back. When, at the 1946 conference in Savannah, Georgia, that launched the International Monetary Fund, Keynes said he hoped no 'malicious fairy' would wreck the proceedings, Frederick Vinson, head of the US delegation, replied: 'I don't mind being called malicious, but I do mind being called a fairy.'

Keynes straddled the worlds of academic life, government, the City and the arts. He chaired National Mutual Life Assurance and the Cambridge Arts Theatre and, as a highly successful investor, made money for both himself and his beloved King's College, lost much of it in the 1929 crash, which he did not see coming, but made it back again, and some more, over the following few years. He was the first chairman of what became the Arts Council. Keynes was no ivory tower economist. He badgered and cajoled politicians and a Treasury that was generally resistant to his ideas. He often set out his views in the pages of *The Times* and publicly took on his critics. In one of Keynes's most famous quotes he takes to task politicians, 'madmen in authority', for being 'slaves of some defunct economist'. Keynes did his best to ensure his ideas were taken up before he was defunct. He lived until 1946, dying at the age of sixty-two, a comparatively short life, and he was in poor health for the last ten years of it. Arguably, his influence was far greater after his death. Now let us see why.

The economic consequences of peace and Churchill

Keynes returned to government service early in 1915, once it became clear that the optimistic view of the First World War, that it would all be over by Christmas 1914, had proved to be badly mistaken. As a Treasury adviser, initially a junior, he rose rapidly and was put in charge of the key task of co-ordinating the country's foreign exchange expenditure on essential wartime imports. Keynes, as he was to demonstrate on many occasions, did not suffer fools gladly, however senior, on one occasion telling Lloyd George, the Prime Minister, that he was talking rubbish. Perhaps surprisingly, this brutal honesty did him little harm with political leaders. Despite being a young man of huge influence, he was evidently frustrated by his wartime service at the Treasury, writing to fellow Bloomsbury group member Duncan Grant in December 1917: 'I work for a government I despise for ends I think criminal.'

This frustration spilled over at the end of the war when, having been assigned to the UK delegation to the Versailles peace conference, he resigned in June 1919 over what he considered to be the dangerous direction it was taking. The issue was the amount of war reparations the defeated Germany should pay to the victorious allies. Keynes argued for no more than £2 billion, still a huge sum at the time, while others were pressing, it appeared successfully, for £24 billion. Although no figure appeared in the Versailles treaty, the implication was that reparations would be very substantial. After his resignation Keynes wrote *The Economic Consequences of the Peace*, criticizing the approach of the allies at Versailles. 'If we aim deliberately at the impoverishment of Central Europe, vengeance, I dare predict, will not limp,' he wrote. Heavy reparations would result initially in a great inflation and eventually in a war 'which will destroy, whoever is victor, the civilisation and progress of our generation'.

Historians have long debated whether Keynes was right. After all, while the Versailles treaty sounded tough, the amount of reparations actually paid by Germany was under £2 billion. However, there was a great inflation, the hyperinflation of the

Weimar era. Inflation is when the general price level is rising. Hyperinflation is when it is rising very rapidly, by more than 50 per cent a month on one definition. Germany in the early 1920s certainly qualified. Between August 1922 and November 1923 prices rose by an average of 322 per cent a month. Thanks to the power of compound interest, this meant that prices at the end of the period were 10.2 billion times those at the start. To put that into perspective, a million marks at the start of the period would be worth less than a pfennig at the end of it. Versailles also established a climate in which the defeated German people felt angry and resentful because, it seemed, the victors were determined to extract full revenge. This was the perfect climate for the rise of Adolf Hitler.

The Economic Consequences of the Peace became a bestseller and Keynes a public figure in Britain and abroad, albeit one often at odds with the political establishment. This was compounded in 1923 when he published *A Tract on Monetary Reform*, in which he argued strongly against a return to the pre-war gold standard. The gold standard, whose heyday was from about 1880 to 1914, was, as its name suggests, a system in which currencies were tied to gold, for both domestic and international purposes. It appealed to 'sound money' bankers and had a certain theoretical simplicity. A country running a balance of payments deficit would in theory have to ship gold out to creditor nations (in practice it was usually moved between different parts of central bank vaults). This loss of gold would, in turn, reduce the supply of money and cut spending at home, thereby correcting the deficit. Keynes, however, had little time for gold, a 'barbarous relic', or for the system. When, against his advice, Britain returned to the gold standard in 1925, the then Chancellor Winston Churchill having taken the decision, Keynes wrote *The Economic Consequences of Mr Churchill*, predicting that the result would be a damagingly overvalued exchange rate and chronic unemployment. Again, he was right. Britain left the gold standard six years later, in 1931, but only after the damage was done.

Saving capitalism from itself

Keynes's criticisms of the conventional wisdom had given him fame, wealth and notoriety but his most constructive contribution was yet to come. The context was the high unemployment of the inter-war years, due to a series of events, including the mistaken desire of countries to return to the gold standard, the Wall Street crash of 1929, and the attempt by countries to protect themselves against global economic woes by putting up trade barriers (so-called 'beggar-my-neighbour' tariffs, such as America's Smoot–Hawley Act of 1930, which pushed tarriffs on US imports to more than 50 per cent). Staple industries such as coal, iron, steel and shipbuilding suffered from chronic over-capacity, hitting parts of Britain particularly hard. As Eric Hobsbawm put it in *Industry and Empire*:

> In 1913–14 about three per cent of the workers in Wales had been unemployed – rather less than the national average. In 1934 – after recovery had begun – thirty-seven per cent of the labour force in Glamorgan, thirty-six per cent of that in Monmouth, were out of work. Two thirds of the men in

Ferndale, three quarters of those in Brynmawr, Dowlais and
Blaina; seventy per cent of those in Merthyr, had nothing to do
except stand at street corners and curse the system which put
them there. The people of Jarrow, in Durham, lived by the
Palmer's shipyard. When it closed in 1933 Jarrow was derelict,
with eight out of ten of its workers jobless, and having like as not
lost all their savings in the crash of the yard, which had so long
been their harsh and noisy universe.

In truth, however, nowhere was immune. In America, without
even Europe's limited pre-war welfare provision, the consequences of mass unemployment were even more severe. The
Great Depression, the mass movement of desperate people in
search of work and food chronicled in John Steinbeck's *The*
Grapes of Wrath, and the failure of thousands of banks and therefore of the supply of credit – on some explanations the cause of
most of the trouble – spoke of a global crisis for capitalism.

It is not true to say that the economists before Keynes had
failed to envisage mass unemployment. In general, though, they
believed that such episodes would be self-correcting. Temporary
spells of unemployment would result in falling wages, which
would increase the demand among employers for workers. The
depression and mass unemployment of the inter-war years
appeared to mark capitalism's nadir. Arguably it was in its death
throes. Many of the intelligentsia in western capitalist societies
saw the crisis as proof that Marx was right, and many saw Marx-
ism as the only solution to it. Smith's 'invisible hand', it seemed,
either was very shaky or no longer worked at all.

Keynes did not. When he wrote *The Economic Consequences of Mr Churchill* he advocated, as an alternative to returning to the gold standard, a programme of government spending, of deliberately running a budget deficit in order to restore economic growth and reduce unemployment. He did so again when appointed to the Macmillan Committee on Finance and Industry in 1929, and whenever he was given the opportunity in his many writings for newspapers and magazines. He was, however, up against a powerful force, the so-called 'Treasury view'. For the guardians of Britain's public finances, Keynes's ideas were dangerously radical. The country, they believed, should run a balanced budget and, where possible, seek to repay debt, not deliberately allow it to build up. Gordon Brown, Chancellor of the Exchequer at the time of writing, tells of finding a pamphlet by Keynes in the Treasury archive. Scrawled across it, by a senior official of the day, was the single word 'inflation'.

The General Theory

Keynes was not deterred. In 1935 he wrote thus to George Bernard Shaw, the playwright: 'I believe myself to be writing a book on economic theory, which will largely revolutionise – not, I suppose, at once but in the course of the next ten years – the way the world thinks about economic problems.' The book, published in 1936, was *The General Theory of Employment, Interest and Money*. Keynes persuaded Macmillan, his publisher, to put it on sale at five shillings (25 pence), believing that, like his earlier works, it would be a bestseller. That was optimistic. Although tens of thousands of copies have been bought by

economists and students over the years, the book was never one
for the general reader. Even economists find it difficult and, in
some respects, confused and contradictory. The great communi-
cator, able to turn out highly readable op-ed articles for *The
Times*, had produced a rather inaccessible book. That, however,
was less important than its message which, as he predicted, did
indeed make people think differently about economic problems
and made it one of the three most important economics books
ever written, along with Smith's *Wealth of Nations* and Marx's
Capital. We have yet to see a fourth to rank alongside these
three, although this is not for want of trying on the part of publishers. When, at the end of the 1990s, the financier George
Soros brought out a book on the 'crisis in global capitalism' (this
was after Asia had hit economic and financial problems), his
publishers claimed, ridiculously, that he had produced the fourth
in a quartet of greats.

To understand Keynes's breakthrough, without getting
bogged down in the complexities of *The General Theory*, it is necessary to return to my 'most useful equation in economics'. This
was the one that said $GDP = C + G + I + X - M$, where C is
consumer spending, G government spending, I investment, X
exports and M imports. Let's ignore X and M for the moment and
concentrate on the others. What happens when C is depressed
because of high unemployment and I is weak because businesses
cannot see any prospect of good times returning? Is it inevitable
that GDP (gross domestic product – the economy as a whole) has
to be weak, the more so because a government seeking to cut its
cloth to suit its means would have to reduce spending in line with

weaker tax revenues? Keynes said no. In these circumstances governments should do precisely the opposite. They should increase spending, particularly on public works (which would mean, on modern definitions, pushing up I, because of higher government investment). By boosting G and the public sector's part of I, GDP would automatically be increased; economic growth would be restored.

Could it really be so simple? After all governments do not create wealth, they merely redistribute the money they raise from taxation. Would not Keynes's solution result, if not in inflation, then in only a temporary fillip, after which the economy would be in even more trouble than before?

Keynes came up with many memorable phrases, 'in the long-run we're all dead' being one of the most famous. Even more pertinent, in this context, is this one from *The General Theory:*

> *If the Treasury were to fill old bottles with banknotes, bury them at suitable depths in disused coalmines which are then filled up with town rubbish, and leave it to private enterprise on well-tried principles of laissez-faire to dig up the notes again (the rights to do so being obtained, of course, by tendering for leases of the note-bearing authority) there need be no more unemployment and, with the help of the repercussions, the real income of the community, and its capital wealth also, would probably become a good deal greater than it actually is.*

The point was that additional government spending, at the right time, would 'prime the pump', triggering higher growth elsewhere in the economy, and the mechanism by which this occurred was probably one of Keynes's most important contributions. The multiplier, already touched upon, ensured that this additional spending by government rippled through the economy. Suppose a public works programme employs 100,000 previously unemployed people at £500 a week. That means an extra £50 million of income. Not all of that will be spent, but if 90 per cent of it is (the workers have an average propensity to consume nine-tenths of their income), there is £45 million of extra spending which generates wages for factory workers, lorry drivers, shop-workers and others. The multiplier, the size and strength of which will be determined by the propensity to consume, also ensures that at least part of the initial injection of public money feeds back to the Treasury in higher tax revenues. The multiplier also offers a strong reason why the 'classical' remedy to unemployment, reducing wages to price workers back into jobs, would not work. Apart from the fact that it is hard to get workers to accept wage cuts, even when prices are falling, wage cuts would, by reducing income, also mean lower spending power, or 'aggregate demand'.

This all sounds fine but was there not a more direct route to stimulating the economy, through cutting interest rates? The next chapter will go into some detail about how this process usually works but Keynes's essential point was that, at the time he was writing, interest rates had lost their potency. In his view a situation could develop where interest rates were as low as the authorities could push them but still too high to stimulate investment, because businesses were too gloomy about prospects – in

Keynes's words, they lacked 'animal spirits'. In other words, it was possible for the economy to be caught in a so-called 'liquidity trap'. Even when interest rates were at their lowest practicable level, perhaps even zero, nobody wanted to borrow. In these circumstances increasing money and credit would not help. All that would happen was that 'idle' balances would build up in banks. If all this sounds a bit far-fetched, Japan since about 1990 has been a living example of an economy caught in a liquidity trap, where interest rates have been effectively cut to zero without stimulating the economy, not least because of falling prices, or deflation. Interestingly, the Japanese government tried 'Keynesian' remedies on a number of occasions, with tax cuts and public works programmes. They did not work, mainly because by keeping interest rates too high at the start of the 1990s the Bank of Japan had allowed a situation of deflation – falling prices (and with it falling confidence) to develop.

There is a lot more to Keynes and *The General Theory* than this brief summary has allowed. Students who delve a little deeper will quickly encounter the so-called 'IS and LM framework', developed by Keynes's followers Sir John Hicks and Alvin Hansen. They will get used to dealing with aggregate demand and aggregate supply. Further reading will reveal a fierce debate about whether Keynes's *General Theory* was in fact general, or merely applied to the special case of the inter-war years. They will also find that he is villain to as many people as he is hero. Keynes may have saved capitalism from itself in the 1930s but to his critics he also ushered in the era of big government and inflationary deficit financing (the Treasury view did not die completely). General readers with the time and interest should read Robert Skidelsky's excellent three-volume biography of Keynes.

Bretton Woods

Before leaving Keynes, it is worth touching briefly on what he did after *The General Theory*. Apart from harrying politicians and debating vigorously with his critics to ensure his ideas were taken up, he was soon, despite a heart attack in 1937, back in active government service. In 1940 he published *How to Pay for the War*, an ingenious plan involving temporary taxation (to prevent a wartime inflation because of the pressure on resources), with a refund to taxpayers once the war was over. There were hints of this in Kingsley Wood's 1941 Budget, but it was more explicitly Keynesian in other respects. Keynes's bigger role was in international negotiations, mainly with the Americans. Rightly, he saw America's wartime ambition as supporting its old ally militarily but, when it came to financial assistance, to do so on terms that would ensure Britain's displacement by the United States as an economic superpower. Keynes saw it coming, both in America's Lend-Lease assistance to wartime Britain and in the US loan that was to tide the economy over in the post-war period. Ironically the defeated European powers, which received Marshall aid, ended up as the stronger economies in the post-war period. Some say that Keynes's failure to change America's approach contributed to his early death.

Before that, he had been Britain's chief negotiator at the Bretton Woods conference in the summer of 1944. Bretton Woods, a sprawling and now once more elegant hotel in the White Mountain National Park in New Hampshire, was chosen as the location for a conference that would shape the world's financial system in the post-war period. It was clear by then that Germany would be defeated, although it was to take nearly another year for the task to be completed, so it was necessary to create a framework that would avoid the problems of the inter-war years. Keynes had a radical plan, the establishment of a world central bank which would create credit and settle payments between countries in its own currency, to be called 'bancor'. Once again he was ahead of his time, too far ahead for the American team and its Treasury secretary, Harry Dexter White. Bretton Woods gave birth to a bank of sorts, the World Bank, and to the International Monetary Fund. It also gave the world the fixed-but-adjustable exchange rate system that was successful for twenty-five years after the war. Currencies were fixed against others, within narrow bands, but could be adjusted in exceptional circumstances. Britain had two such adjustments under the system, devaluing the pound in both 1949 (from $4.00 to $2.80) and 1967 (from $2.80 to $2.40). Gallingly for Keynes, this system had echoes of the gold standard he so despised. Called the gold exchange standard, it survived until America, under Richard Nixon, suspended the convertibility of dollars into gold in 1971.

Although Keynes did not get his way at Bretton Woods his contribution was immense. Some say the international monetary system he envisaged would still be in place today, but who knows? As with everything else he did, he was impossible to ignore.

**
*

And now, as Keynes leaves us with a flourish, it is time to come right back up to date. The economic picture is almost complete and the guests are feeling rather full. It is time to talk about something that often comes up at the dinner table, and can be the cause of indigestion – bread in common parlance, money to you and me.

11

Bread and money

Sooner or later, vulgar though it may be, most dinner-table conversations get round to money. It is perhaps surprising that we have come so far without talking about it explicitly, although we have explored those other favourite topics – mortgages and house prices. Without money, after all, what would we be, mere primitives exchanging half a dozen cows for a new wife? Cattle, in fact, played an important part in the development of money. Chattels, as in 'wife and chattels', and capital, as in capital investment, or even the name of Marx's most famous work, come from the same Old English roots as cattle. Some apparently primitive societies used money in a highly sophisticated way, even if their money was rather different from ours. On the island of Yap in the South Pacific very heavy stones were used as money, which had the virtue of making them hard to steal, while in the New Hebrides they used feather money, and what could be easier to carry around? In Borneo, by tradition, human skulls were used as money, and if this sounds gruesome to us, it was because they happened to be their most prized possessions. Whales' teeth were used in Fiji. Manillas, forms of ornamental metal jewellery, were used in West Africa as recently as 1949. Even in modern economies, in particular circumstances, other things have replaced conventional money. Cigarettes, or perhaps these days drugs, are the main currency within prisons, where cash is of limited use. Cigarettes also became the currency of choice during the great European hyperinflations of the twentieth century, particularly in Germany. Cigarettes, it seemed, held their value better than money.

It can be fun, if only on a rainy afternoon, to trace the way in which currencies came to have their names. A pound was called a pound for fairly obvious reasons – it was the amount of silver that weighed a Roman pound, or *libra* (hence lira as well, and the fact that the letter 'l' was used to denote both). A mark was also a measurement of weight – two-thirds of a pound. A drachma meant a handful of grain. The unit of currency in medieval Britain was the penny, whose symbol until decimalization in 1971 was the letter 'd', from the Latin *denarius*, which spawned many currency names, notably the dinar. Quite why the pound became the pound sterling from about the twelfth century, maybe a little earlier, is less certain. We know that sterling originally described a penny, so one pound sterling was actually a pound of sterlings. Why sterling? One suggestion is that it was a corruption of 'starling', another that it derived from 'easterlings', northeastern European merchants. Nicholas

Mayhew, a coin expert from the Ashmolean Museum at Oxford who has written widely on the subject, favours the explanation that it derives from 'ster', a Middle English word implying strength and stability.

What does money do? We may wonder. Carl Menger, in his classic 1892 article 'On the Origins of Money', conceded that the fact that every individual and every business 'should be ready to exchange his goods for little metal discs, or for documents representing the latter' appeared to be 'downright mysterious'. The paragraph above tells most of the story. Money's primary purpose is as a medium of exchange. Therefore it has to be generally acceptable. Cigarette money would not be much use in a nation of 95 per cent non-smokers. Acceptability is more important, in general, than something many people get hung up on – whether a particular form of money is legal tender. Legal tender simply means what people are required to accept, under the law, in payment of debts. That can vary. A penny is legal tender in most uses but anybody trying to settle a £1,000 bill in pennies could legitimately be refused. For generations, kilt-wearing Scotsmen down for the rugby have been outraged when London taxi drivers have refused to accept their Scottish banknotes. The cabbies are perfectly within their rights. While generally accepted north of the border, Scottish banknotes are not legal tender even in Scotland.

Money must also be a store of value, which is one reason why durable metals were used as money, and why it took time for paper money to be trusted. There are plenty of examples of food being used as money but, like any perishable good, it suffers from a certain basic disadvantage. Money should also be a unit of account. As long as people are able to assess the value of things in terms of the number of cigarettes they would cost, there is nothing to stop cigarette money acting as a unit of account. In his article, Menger also explained why precious metals were peculiarly suited to act as money. They were, he pointed out, widely coveted and scarce in relation to the demand for them. You might turn up your nose at accepting a plastic token as payment, but never gold or silver.

From money to Mastercard

The story of banking is older than that of money itself, or at least coinage. In Mesopotamia or ancient Egypt, banks were storehouses for grain or other commodities. Receipts, promises to pay, issued for the deposit or transfers of grain became used as currency. Paper money, for that is what it was, therefore goes back a long way. Ancient civilizations had relatively sophisticated banking systems. We know from the Greek and Roman coinage that has survived that the amount of money in circulation was considerable. We also know that the coinage was only part of a more extensive monetary framework, including banks. The history of money is not, however, a smooth one. Paper money appears to have died out when the Roman empire crumbled, and was not revived, at least in Europe, until about the twelfth century, given an impetus by the crusades – when a way had to be found to make payments for supplies and equipment and to pay allies. Banking services, already developing rapidly in Italian city-states such as Rome and Genoa, became international. If we now fast-forward to England in the seventeenth century, and the Civil War (1642–51), wealthy people stored their jewellery, bullion and other valuables in the secure strong-boxes or safes of goldsmiths. As in ancient Egypt, paper money was the consequence of such deposits. A cheque – an instruction to the goldsmith to pay – could effect a transfer of money from one person to another. Receipts given on the deposit of valuables could be exchanged. By about 1660 these receipts had become banknotes. Similar developments occurred in other countries.

So far, however, there is nothing about paper money, apart from the fact that it is lighter and more convenient to carry, that distinguishes it from the gold and other valuables that it represents. That difference started to occur when the goldsmiths began to realize that most of the valuables in their safes never left the premises. As long as people were confident that when the time came they would be able to withdraw their gold, they were happy to conduct their business in gold's paper form. And as long as the goldsmiths could be confident that not everybody was going to want to take out their gold at the same time, they could issue many more banknotes – drawn on gold – than there were quantities of the precious metal in their vaults. It sounds like trickery but it is the basis of modern banking. The Scotsman John Law, at one time described as the richest man in the world, took this process forward in the early eighteenth century by persuading the French royal court to adopt what was then the most sophisticated paper money system in the world. Because the scheme was linked to shares in the Mississippi Company, a highly speculative venture, the experiment ended disastrously. But the paper money era was born.

Except in circumstances like these, the issue of paper money should not be confused with the fact that banks still have to ensure that their deposits and loans are in rough balance. The same applies, of course, to cash now. I remember being quite shocked as a child when I discovered that if everybody wanted to take his or her notes and coin out of the bank at the same time there would not be nearly enough to go round. Sometimes, of course, depositors test that process to the limit, when there is a run on the bank, which is when the central bank has to step in as lender of last resort, often supported by other banks keen to maintain confidence in the system. When there is a run on the system as a whole, the central bank can respond by printing more money. The result of that is likely to be inflation, of which more below.

The process by which banks expand the amount of 'money' in the economy by building on a relatively small monetary base is known as 'credit creation'. The amount of money that is in circulation is, in turn, determined by what is known as the 'money multiplier'. If, by custom and practice, banks find that they need to hold 10 per cent of loans and deposits in the form of cash, the money multiplier is 10 – there is ten times the amount of money in circulation, cheques drawn on the bank for example, as there is hard cash. In practice, most countries operate on the basis of an even smaller proportion of cash – certainly less than 10 per cent – and on money multipliers of between 10 and 20. A central bank that wanted to slow lending in the economy, perhaps because the economy was in danger of overheating, growing too fast, and running into an inflation problem, could impose tighter 'reserve requirements' – increasing the amount of cash (and deposits with the central bank) that the banks have to hold.

What about plastic money? Apart from the fact that debit and credit cards have led people to economize even further on the use of cash, they are just an extension of the earlier variations of non-cash money described above. A debit card is simply a plastic version of a cheque. A credit card is slightly different, being a loan, usually a short-term one, from the bank to its retail customer, while the store receiving a payment usually has to pay the bank a merchant's fee for the privilege of doing so (although they would also typically pay the bank for processing a cheque). The underlying principle is, however, no different from other forms of credit creation.

Money and monetary policy

That's enough history, certainly enough ancient history. Everybody knows what money is, but what is monetary policy? Every month, for two days, nine men and women gather together in a special committee room deep inside the Bank of England overlooked by a portrait of Montagu Norman, one of its legendary governors, who went a little peculiar towards the end of his twenty-four-year (1920–44) term. These nine are collectively known as the monetary policy committee (MPC). While the Chancellor of the Exchequer and his Treasury team are sorting out fiscal policy in SW1 – Whitehall – the MPC is fixing monetary policy in EC3, the City. This now seems entirely natural but, as most people will be aware, is a very recent phenomenon. Gordon Brown came to the Treasury in early May 1997 after Labour's election victory on an apparent policy of seeing how the Bank performed for a while before considering the question of independence. Within five days he had apparently seen enough. The Bank was given responsibility for monetary policy, for setting interest rates at the appropriate level to achieve the government's inflation target, 2.5 per cent.

Why was this such a big deal? After all, similar arrangements had worked in America, where the Federal Reserve System has a Federal Open Market Committee to set interest rates, and in Germany, where the Bundesbank, which came into being in the 1950s after the second of Germany's post-war hyperinflations, had established a deserved reputation for sound money and low inflation. The Bundesbank, in turn, provided the model for the European Central Bank. New Zealand and Australia had established broadly similar arrangements. South Africa was in the process of doing so. It was a big deal in Britain because no previous Prime Minister, even if urged to do it by his Chancellor of the Exchequer, had considered that central bank independence was appropriate for Britain. Britain is a nation of homeowners: nearly 70 per cent of all property is owner-occupied. It is also a nation of small and medium-sized firms. Most homeowners and small and medium-sized firms borrow on the basis of variable interest rates. If interest rates double, they feel the impact immediately. Despite strong academic evidence that independent central banks were associated with better economic performance – low inflation, greater stability and somewhat faster economic growth – Britain's politicians had always considered interest rates too important to hand over to unelected bankers. To understand why it happened, it is necessary to review briefly the catalogue of errors that preceded Bank of England independence.

The seven ages of monetary policy

There are the seven ages of man and there are the seven ages of modern UK monetary policy. It is a good way of looking at the trials and errors that got us to where we are today. Other countries have groped for the ideal monetary policy, although few have done so as ineptly as Britain. If we go back a quarter of a century or so, to the 1970s, this was a time of enormous turbulence for the world economy and near-disaster for Britain. It is also my first age of modern UK monetary policy – reluctant monetarism. In 1976 a near-bankrupt government had to call in the International Monetary Fund. This was the occasion for the burying of post-war Keynesianism. Peter Jay, sometime British ambassador to Washington and economics editor of *The Times* and the BBC, drafted a speech for his father-in-law, James Callaghan, for the 1976 Labour Party conference, which contained the immortal words 'I tell you in all candour that you can't spend your way out of recession'. The IMF's prescription contained two main elements. It insisted on sharp cuts in public spending – the biggest by any government in the post-war period. And it forced the government to adopt monetary targets, to control the money supply or, more particularly, two measures of 'money', one called sterling M3 and the other domestic credit expansion. There is no need to worry about the detail of what these were. The essential point was a simple one. To stabilize the economy and to control inflation (which had risen above 26 per cent during 1975) it was necessary to control the money supply. There will be more on this when we meet Milton Friedman in the next chapter but the basis of this policy was straightforward – just as you cannot drive a car without petrol, you cannot have inflation without money. The faster money is printed and credit allowed to grow, the higher will be inflation. Targeting the money supply was by no means trouble-free. The Labour government found, as many governments have, that it was not possible to control the money supply and the exchange rate simultaneously. By the time it lost the 1979 election inflationary pressures were starting to build up strongly. Even so, this reluctant monetarism helped to save the economy.

In 1979 we had the second age – willing monetarism – under a Thatcher government philosophically committed to controlling the money supply as a means of limiting inflation. Despite being willing acolytes of Friedman, the Conservatives chose a 'broad' monetary target, sterling M3, which he would not have recommended. They then proceeded to undertake other policy actions, notably the abolition of exchange controls (limits on the amount of currency and capital that could be taken in and out of the country) and of the Bank of England 'corset' (controls on the banks' lending), which made it impossible to hit the targets for sterling M3. To this day many people think monetarism has something to do with public spending cuts. This was because the

Thatcher government's choice of money supply target was linked to the level of public borrowing, and therefore the amount of government spending. This phase of willing monetarism lasted two or three years, before giving way to the third age – pragmatic monetarism.

By the early 1980s Charles Goodhart, then chief monetary adviser to the Bank of England, had come up with Goodhart's Law, a kind of Murphy's Law for economics. This did not say that if you drop a piece of toast it is bound to fall buttered side down but, rather, that any measure of the money supply you try to target will automatically become subject to distortions that make it hard to control. So the Conservative government adopted a more relaxed approach, making it clear that they still believed in controlling the money supply but also choosing to target a range of measures and not losing too much sleep if one or more of them missed the target. This approach worked pretty well. From 1982 until 1985 Britain had reasonable economic growth, albeit alongside high unemployment, and low inflation.

Unfortunately, sterling, the traditional Achilles heel of the UK economy, was still subject to periodic crises. January 1985, not long after I had joined *The Times* as economics correspondent, began with interest rates at 9.5 per cent and ended at 14 per cent, sterling having come within a whisker of one-to-one parity with the dollar in the process. These days we get excited when interest rates change by half a percentage point in a month. And so, in about 1985, Nigel Lawson, the then Chancellor, became rather keen on taking sterling into the European exchange rate mechanism – the system of 'fixed-but-adjustable' exchange rates in Europe that had come into being in 1979 as a forerunner to an eventual single currency. When Thatcher rebuffed him, he developed an alternative. Under the cloak of international efforts to stabilize currencies, the so-called G5 (Group of Five) and G7 (Group of Seven) Plaza and Louvre accords, that alternative was unofficial exchange rate targeting – shadowing the Deutschmark, my fourth age of monetary policy. How much was this responsible for the boom and bust of the late 1980s? Quite a lot. The earlier pragmatism was replaced by dogmatism, with dogma directed at preventing the pound from rising above three D-marks. The lessons of the early 1980s were forgotten, a kind of Goodhart's Law applied to the exchange rate.

My fifth age is official targeting of the exchange rate – the ERM period. John Major was more successful than Lawson in persuading Thatcher of the virtues of joining the ERM, partly because he convinced her that it was the route to lower interest rates. And so, when in October 1990 it was announced that the pound would be joining the ERM at an exchange rate of DM2.95, it was also announced that interest rates would be reduced at the same time, from 15 to 14 per cent. The problem with ERM membership was, however, the opposite of the one Major suggested. Far from being a route to lower interest rates, it blocked interest rate cuts at the very time they were needed. The combination of what was seen as a high exchange rate and the persistence of high interest rates meant that the period of ERM membership coincided with the 1990–92 recession, the longest in Britain's post-war history. There was an additional complication.

As a result of the pressures created by the unification of East and West Germany, German interest rates were higher than usual, and they set the pattern for the rest of Europe including, at the time, Britain. By the summer of 1992 the Conservative government, having narrowly won re-election in April 1992 (this time with Major as Prime Minister) was hanging on for dear life in the ERM. On 16 September 1992 the game was up. 'Black' Wednesday to the headline writers, 'White' or 'Golden' Wednesday to others, this was the day the Bank of England ran out of the reserves needed to prop up the pound within the system. It bought large quantities of sterling with its own foreign currency but, thanks to George Soros and other speculators, it was to no avail.

The sixth age came after Black Wednesday and sterling's departure from the ERM, and it can be called quasi Bank of England independence. In putting together a monetary policy framework out of the ruins of the ERM failure, and in doing it both quickly and in an environment where it seemed the government could fall at any moment, the Treasury and the then Chancellor, Norman Lamont, performed a minor miracle. That framework, adopting an inflation target instead of money supply or exchange rate targets, requiring the Bank of England to produce a quarterly inflation report, and getting the Bank to advise openly and regularly on interest rate changes (this became the 'Ken and Eddie show' after Kenneth Clarke, Lamont's successor, and Eddie George, the Bank governor) was enormously successful. It paved the way for the 1990s to be a period, after the disasters at the start, of non-inflationary growth, the holy grail of economic policy.

From there it was a relatively short step to giving the Bank the job.

The seventh age is thus operational independence for the Bank in which the Bank sets rates to meet an inflation target, 2.5 per cent, set by the government. Is this the final resting place for monetary policy? One is tempted to say yes, and it certainly feels more permanent than its predecessors. There are, however, a couple of possibilities for change. The first one would be if, within the existing system, the Bank was not subject to a specific inflation target but was given the broad brief of achieving economic stability, of the sort the Bundesbank used to have and the Federal Reserve has. A second possibility, of course, is membership of Europe's monetary union, the euro. Here, the governor of the Bank would simply become a voting member of a large European central bank council. That would look like a permanent resting place for monetary policy, although many – including some in the Treasury and the Bank – are not prepared to give up the present arrangements without a fight.

How does monetary policy work?

When the Bank of England's monetary policy committee meets each month it is to make one of three decisions. To raise interest rates, to lower them, or to leave them the same. For all central banks leaving interest rates unchanged is the most common decision. To raise them or to lower them the economists and bankers on the committee need to be convinced that enough has changed since they last met to warrant a shift. That does not mean rate changes are a rarity. Most central banks prefer to operate on the principle of 'little and often' in altering rates, rather than go in for the big, bold gesture, although even in its relatively short history of independence the Bank did not adjust rates for twelve whole months between February 2000 and February 2001.

What is it about interest rates that gives them this influence on the economy? After all, the economy is made up of savers and borrowers, and their savings and borrowings roughly equal one another, so surely the net effect of a change in interest rates is zero. A rise in interest rates is good for savers but is a blow for borrowers, and vice versa for a fall. One man's meat is another man's poison. In fact it is a little more complicated than that, although not greatly so. The way in which interest rates affect the economy is called the 'transmission mechanism of monetary policy' and there is a very good paper on the Bank's website (www.bankofengland.co.uk) with precisely this title.

Let us consider, first, what happens when the MPC decides to raise interest rates. It would do this because it believed there was a real danger of inflation rising above the 2.5 per cent target – the inflation rate deemed by the government to be consistent with a stable economy. The first and most obvious effect on individuals would be to make saving more attractive by increasing the interest rates on saving accounts, and borrowing less attractive because it has become more expensive. People with savings are happy, because their income has risen. People with borrowings, and 80 per cent of borrowings in Britain are in the form of mortgages, find that their monthly payments have increased. The consequence for them is that they have less to spend on other things. Why is this not exactly offset by greater spending by the savers whose income has risen? Here, it is necessary to make an assumption that is fortunately supported by the facts. It is that savers have a lower tendency to spend any extra income, a lower marginal propensity to consume, than borrowers. Why should this be? Under the life-cycle hypothesis, which we have already encountered, people's lives divide naturally into periods of spending and periods of saving. In general, those aged forty and under are high spenders and low savers. From forty or so until retirement people save relatively more and spend relatively less; they are also less likely to have heavy borrowings. On retirement they start to draw down those savings. A cut in interest rates therefore has the neat effect of putting more money into the hands of those people who are most likely to spend it, those with high mortgages relative to income. A rise in rates has the opposite impact. There are other consequences for individuals. Higher interest rates will tend to make people think there are more difficult times on the way, and perhaps their job is at risk. They may also be associated with slower growth (or a fall) in house prices and the stock market, thereby affecting wealth. Wealth, and this distinction is not always made clear, particularly by journalists, is the *stock* of assets built up over time. Income is the *flow* of new money coming in. Roughly half of individual wealth in Britain is in housing, with most of the remainder held (often indirectly through pension funds) in stock market-related investments.

So, higher interest rates will, through these various routes, tend to slow consumer spending, while lower rates will tend to speed it up. Similar principles apply, although in a slightly different form, when it comes to firms. As the Bank of England itself puts it:

> *An increase in the official interest rate will have a direct effect on all firms that rely on bank borrowing or on loans of any kind linked to short-term money-market interest rates. A rise in interest rates increases borrowing costs. The rise in interest rates reduces the profits of such firms and increases the return that firms will require from new investment projects, making it less likely they will start them. Interest costs affect the cost of holding inventories [stocks of components or finished goods], which are often financed by bank loans. Higher interest costs also make it less likely that the affected firms will hire more staff, and more likely that they will reduce employment or hours worked. In contrast, when interest rates are falling, it is cheaper for firms to finance investment in new plant and equipment, and more likely that they will expand their labour force.*

From growth to inflation

This is all very well, but where does inflation come into it? So far, all we have seen is that interest rates affect the growth of the economy, either for good or bad. The essential requirement, therefore, is that growth and inflation are linked, and for this we need another couple of tools. The first is the notion of the economy's long run, or 'trend' growth rate, which in Britain's case is thought to be 2.5 per cent. The second is what is called the 'output gap'. This needs explanation. Suppose that, year in, year out, the UK economy grew by 2.5 per cent a year. The economy would be growing exactly on trend and the output gap would be zero. Now suppose there are three consecutive years of zero growth. The consequences of this would be rising unemployment and spare capacity. It would also be low inflation. The more slack there is in the economy the weaker, other things being equal, are the inflationary pressures. Output would have dropped significantly below trend. An output gap, economy-wide spare capacity, would have been created. In this case three years of growth at 5 per cent a year would be required to get the economy back on track, and the Bank need not worry too much about such a rapid rate of expansion. If we take another situation, however, when three years of 5 per cent growth started from the point when the economy was already on trend, it would be a different story. The effect would be a sharp drop in unemployment, probably serious skill shortages, and pressures on capacity elsewhere. A 'negative' output gap – in other words an economy operating well above its cumulative trend – would have emerged. Higher inflation would be expected and the Bank's response would be to raise interest rates to get the economy back on trend as quickly as possible.

These things can never, of course, be purely mechanical. Successful monetary policy requires skill and touch, as well as an ability to interpret the economic numbers. But this, in a nutshell, is the way it works. A rapidly growing economy which is at or above trend is likely to be heading for higher inflation, and a hike in interest rates should be the policy response, and vice versa.

There is one other transmission route from interest rate changes to inflation to consider, and that is the exchange rate. In Britain's case, because of the openness of the economy (exports and imports are each the equivalent of just under a third of GDP), the pound's performance has traditionally been very important. Many of the best-laid plans of governments, as we saw in the seven ages of monetary policy, have been upset by sterling's unwillingness to behave. In normal circumstances, a rise in UK interest rates should push the pound higher, while a reduction will have the opposite effect. This is because, in theory, international investors are always scanning the world to look for the best returns. If the Bank of England pushes up rates, that is a signal to those investors to shift their money to London. It does not always work out like this. In September 1992 even 15 per cent interest rates did not push the pound higher, because the international financial community was convinced sterling was about to be devalued (so holders of sterling would have been left much poorer). Leaving such circumstances aside, and assuming higher interest rates do indeed lead to a stronger pound, it is not hard to see why this should be associated with lower inflation. There is a direct link to prices, because when sterling rises against other currencies, the effect is to reduce the cost of imports, right through from commodities to cars. There is also an indirect effect, via growth. A higher pound makes exports more expensive and therefore hurts exporting companies, while benefiting firms in other countries (those selling to Britain or competing with UK exports in other markets). These effects can be powerful, although the size of them depends on circumstances. With sterling's 1992 departure from the ERM and its subsequent large depreciation, many feared a sharp rise in inflation. (A depreciation is when a currency slides lower until it finds its level, a devaluation is when it is moved by the authorities from one fixed rate to a lower one. The last formal devaluation in Britain was in 1967, when sterling was devalued from $2.80 to $2.40.) It did not happen, because the economy was just recovering from a severe recession. There was, in other words, a large output gap.

Whatever happened to monetarism?

There is plenty more that could be said about money but it is nearly time to move on. There is one more set of guests to entertain us, and we should not keep them waiting too long. Since one of them is Milton Friedman, however, we should briefly address one question. Why is monetarism, so much in vogue in the 1980s, now barely mentioned?

The roots of monetarism go back to the birth of modern economics. Its central tenet is simplicity itself. The faster the growth in the amount of money in circulation the more rapid, other things being equal, the rate of price rises – inflation. David Hume, a contemporary of Adam Smith, wrote in his 1750 essay 'Of Money' about the effects of an increase in the quantity of money in circulation: 'At first, no alteration is perceived, by degrees the price rises, first of one commodity, then of another, till the whole at last reaches a just proportion with the quantity of specie which is in the kingdom.' The language is a little archaic but the message is relatively clear, although Alfred Marshall, Keynes's Cambridge teacher, perhaps put it a little more succinctly 150 years later. 'If everything else remains the same,' he wrote, 'then there is this direct relation between the volume of currency and the level of prices, that if one is increased by 10 per cent, the other will also be increased by 10 per cent.'

Until 1914 few economists challenged the basis of monetarism, the quantity theory of money. The pre-First World War gold standard, under which paper money was backed up by and convertible into gold, both underlined money's pre-eminence as an economic lever and institutionalized monetarist-type arrangements. Under the gold standard unreliable politicians and central bankers were constrained from expanding the money supply too rapidly. It was something of a monetarist paradise.

So what happened? Two things – Keynes and the Great Depression. Keynes emphasized the power of fiscal policy and explained how monetary policy could lose its effectiveness – it could be as effective as 'pushing on a piece of string'. As importantly, there was a real-life example in America during the depression years. Actually, there was a good monetarist explanation for the depression and deflation (falling prices) of the 1930s. America's Federal Reserve, in a lesson imprinted indelibly on the minds of every subsequent Fed chairman, allowed too many banks to fail, producing a sharp contraction in the money supply. Interestingly, one big debate at the time of writing is on how to rescue the Japanese economy from its long slump and deflation. Having tried the Keynesian remedy, with repeated public works programmes, Japan may have to opt for a monetarist one – a big expansion of money and credit.

In some countries monetarism did not go away at all, in others it did so only temporarily. In the 1950s, when the legendary Bundesbank came into being, it used a combination of a monetarist approach and the German folk memory of two hyperinflations to achieve more than forty years of low inflation. Britain and America were much keener on the Keynesian approach and on 'fine-tuning'. It took until 1979 and the election of Margaret Thatcher for a British government to embrace monetarism willingly and then, as noted above, with mixed results.

Was monetarism right or wrong? Few economists would dispute that there is a relationship between the money supply and inflation, although many would question whether that relationship could ever be precise. For one thing, the speed money circulates at around the economy (the technical term is 'velocity of circulation') will affect the pass-through from money to inflation. For another, the lags between changes in the money supply and inflation are, as monetarists concede, 'long and variable'. The link between money and inflation can also be affected by changes in the financial system and in the use of money. A rapid shift towards a cashless society would not mean there was no useful message in the rate at which cash is growing, but it would mean that such information would need to be interpreted with care. Others would argue that there is nothing magical about the link between money and inflation. When the economy is picking up, one of the first things to happen is that individuals and companies start to borrow more. Measures of the money supply therefore start rising, ahead of any increase in inflation. The driving force of inflation is faster growth in the economy, not faster money supply growth. Every year there is a big rise in the money supply in the autumn, the critics of monetarism say, which is followed by a frenetic bout of Christmas shopping. Nobody, however, would pretend that the increase in the money supply has 'caused' Christmas.

We'll leave them to argue this out. The point is that, in setting interest rates, most central banks these days take note of what is happening to the money supply but are not slaves to it. The idea that monetary policy could operate on automatic pilot – simply set targets for the money supply and make sure you stick to them – has been discredited. Money matters, but so do plenty of other things.

**

Time to move on. Readers may have noticed that, with the exception of the occasional sideways glance at the French and the bulky presence of the German-born Karl Marx, British economists have dominated. All that, sadly, is about to change. Britain in 1945 discovered that she had not just lost an empire. She also lost her dominance of economics to the new superpower, America.

12

Just desserts – the Americans

Why did economics come to be dominated by America, and Americans, after 1945? With Europe ravaged by war and oppression, America's universities became a haven for European intellectuals displaced from their homelands. This was not just true in economics, of course, but it provided a significant boost for the subject. America, too, had fewer hang-ups about economics, which perhaps has something to do with the nature of its society. In Britain economics had a long battle against intellectual snobs who insisted that it was not quite a proper subject. Eric Roll, in his *A History of Economic Thought*, sees it as a natural consequence of Britain's displacement as a global economic power:

It is not surprising that the relative preponderance of English

> *economic thought should decline once England ceased to be the only important capitalist country. Nor is it surprising that the emergence of the United States as the leading capitalist country should have coincided with a very considerable increase of American theoretical activity. Today the accumulated and current output of American economic literature is vast; and it is only barely an exaggeration to say that the study of economics, as we have become accustomed to it over the last hundred years, has its most congenial home in the United States.*

America's modern-day control of economics is not in doubt. The Nobel Prize for economics (strictly, the Swedish Central Bank prize, judged by the Nobel Committee), was instituted in 1969. At the time of writing, forty-nine economists had won it (some sharing with others). America's dominance is underlined by the fact that thirty-two of these were American. Britain, incidentally, is in second place with seven Nobel laureates in economics, followed by Sweden and Norway, with two each, and Canada, India, France, Russia, the Netherlands and Germany, each with one. Canada's winner, incidentally, was Robert Mundell, who has plied his trade in US universities and is often thought of as American. America's prizewinners have included Milton Friedman, Paul Samuelson, Kenneth Arrow, Herbert Simon, Robert Solow, Gary Becker, John Nash and Robert Lucas.

From an early stage in America there were few doubts about the value of economics, although the determination of many practitioners of the subject to turn it into a fully fledged, mathematically based science also meant that it became very different from the 'political economy' of most of the classical British economists and even their twentieth-century successors. This is not to say America invented mathematical economics – Alfred Marshall's approach was highly mathematical – but American economists developed it. It is not to say, either, that there were no great American economists before 1945. One was John Bates Clark (1847–1938), whose work on wages and income distribution, and in other areas, followed the 'marginalist' approach of, for example, Britain's Marshall. Better known these days, however, is one of the greatest of all, Irving Fisher (1867–1947).

Fisher and money

Irving Fisher, to some the best American economist ever, was a fascinating character. He became a millionaire not through economics but through inventing for his own use, and patenting, the index card system we now know as the Rolodex. Fisher set up a company to manufacture it, sold it on, and by the 1920s was sitting on a fortune. Unfortunately, such was his belief in the 'new era' for the American economy of the 1920s – something like the new economy of information technology of the 1990s – he failed to see the 1929 crash coming. 'Stock prices have reached what looks like a permanently high plateau,' he wrote in mid-October 1929. His reputation and his fortune suffered when the market crashed, and he never really recovered.

Fisher's two big contributions were on the way we think about the rate of interest and, in particular, money. Two books, *The Rate of Interest* in 1907 and *The Theory of Interest* in 1930, established what became the conventional framework for thinking about interest, which as he put it in the earlier book 'is an index of the community's preference for a dollar of present income over a dollar of future income'. The higher the rate of interest, in other words, the more we will be prepared to forgo spending now in favour of spending later. This time aspect was crucial. It explained why, in normal circumstances, real (after-inflation) interest rates have to be positive – otherwise any money saved is eroded in value by inflation. The 'Fisher equation' showed that the level of interest rates at any one time was made up of the real interest rate plus expected inflation. Fisher also demonstrated the role of interest rates in investment decisions, and how different rates could alter the ranking of, say, competing projects, depending also partly on the payback period for such projects.

His most famous contribution was, however, what is known as the quantity theory of money (sometimes called the 'Fisher identity' or, confusingly, the 'Fisher equation of exchange'). This may be the point to relax the 'no equation' rule of this book just once more. Thinking back to the monetarism of the previous chapter, Fisher turned what had essentially been an often wordy and imprecise description of the relationship between money and prices into something that modern economists can use. The quantity theory is simple enough: $MV = PT$. In it, M is the amount of money in circulation (the stock of money), V is the speed, or velocity, at which it circulates around the economy. P is the level of prices and T the number of transactions. On the simplifying assumption that V is fairly constant and T does not change much either (assumptions, it should be said, that have caused monetarists a lot of trouble), a change in M – the stock of money – results in a change in P, prices. As Fisher put it: 'The level of prices varies in direct proportion with the quantity of money in circulation, provided that the velocity of money and the volume of trade which it is obliged to perform are not changed.' Control money and you will control inflation. This, of course, was the basis both of Margaret Thatcher's monetarism and the version pursued in America under Ronald Reagan in the early 1980s by Paul Volcker at the Federal Reserve Board.

The Keynesian economist as bestseller – Paul Samuelson

As any author does, I have high hopes for this book, but I can safely predict that it will not sell as many copies as Samuelson's *Economics*. It was first published in 1948, when he was thirty-three, and has been through numerous editions since. There can be few students of economics, business studies or other related subjects who have not pored over a copy. '*Economics* was destined to become the most successful textbook ever published in any field,' writes Mark Skousen, in his *The Making of Modern Economics*.

> *Sixteen editions have sold more than four million copies and have been translated into over forty languages. No other textbook, including those of Jean-Baptiste Say, John Stuart Mill and Alfred Marshall, can compare. Samuelson's* Economics *survived a half-century of dramatic changes in the world economy and the economics profession: peace and war,*

boom and bust, inflation and deflation, Republicans and
Democrats, and an array of new economic theories.

Other textbooks have come and gone. British students of my
generation will recall Richard Lipsey's *An Introduction to Positive*
Economics. Later students will have benefited from one of the
many editions of Begg, Dornbusch and Fischer's *Economics*.
Samuelson, however, provided the template. He may have been
lucky with his bestseller. It emerged when there was a gap in the
market, none of the existing textbooks of the time having
caught up properly with Keynesian economics. It started life as
course notes for students at Harvard and MIT (Massachusetts
Institute of Technology), the latter institution being where
Samuelson made his name. He was, however, much more than
someone who just popularized Keynes. Like other eminent
American economists such as Alvin Hansen, one of Samuelson's
teachers, he gave us what became known as the Keynesian
framework. This was not just a question of interpretation. In his
General Theory of 1936, Keynes was often imprecise and contradictory. The American Keynesians, in particular, made it coherent.

They also made it very mathematical. Samuelson was a noted
mathematician, like most of the top post-war American economists, and made no secret of his view of the shortcomings of
Britain's 'literary' tradition of economic exposition. If economics was to be regarded as a grown-up science, it had to start using
the language of science. What this meant, of course, was that
academic economics became a closed society with its own in-

built restrictive practices – anybody who did not understand the language and code could not hope to enter. Articles in economic journals became impenetrable to even the intelligent layman, although Samuelson would argue, correctly, that this was not the case for his textbook.

Samuelson gave us in diagrammatical and equation form what most would recognize as standard Keynesian analysis, using the national income identity (otherwise known as the most useful equation in economics). This is the one from back in our main course that shows that gross domestic product consists of consumer spending, investment, government spending and net exports (exports less imports), in other words $Y = C + I + G + X - M$. He also developed the consumption function – consumer spending rises in proportion to income – and other underpinnings of Keynesian economic policy. Keynesian policy was, in essence, that on the many occasions when the market fails to generate full employment, the government should do so. Samuelson advised John F. Kennedy during his 1960–63 administration. A couple of examples of his contributions are worth pulling out. One is the paradox of thrift, referred to in Keynes's *General Theory* but only properly developed by Samuelson. This was that, while additional savings to fund productive investment would normally be regarded as unequivocally good, that extra saving, if it reduced consumption and therefore aggregate demand, could be damaging, even to investment. If all businessmen see is a slowing economy because people are saving more and spending less, why should they invest?

Another of his contributions, the 'balanced budget multiplier', shows the subtlety of Keynesian economics at work. A balanced budget implies that the government is neither adding nor subtracting from demand in the economy. Government policy is neutral. But Samuelson demonstrated that whether or not it was neutral depended on the detail of the government's fiscal policy. A government that introduced 'tax and spend' policies, raising tax to increase public spending by the same amount would, while still sticking to a balanced budget, boost the economy. How so? Because government spending provides the economy with a greater stimulus – it goes directly into extra demand for goods, services and people. Tax, however, is subject to various 'leakages', for example into savings or imports. Thus £1 billion spent by government will, through the multiplier, have a bigger impact than £1 billion used for tax cuts. By implication, £1 billion raised through extra taxes and spent on public services will provide a net stimulus.

Such thinking is no longer fashionable, although it still has its followers, not least those who grew up on Samuelson's textbook. But it was hugely influential in the 1950s, 1960s and much of the 1970s.

Friedman and the backlash
There was a time, not so long ago, when the entire economic debate could be characterized as a battle between monetarists and Keynesians. As bitter as any religious dispute or deep-seated sporting rivalry, there was a schism that ran right through the economics profession. Pragmatism may be the fashionable and appropriate position to adopt now but in the 1980s that was not

allowed. Either you were a monetarist or you were a Keynesian, and never the twain did meet. In 1981, famously, 364 Keynesian economists from British universities signed a round-robin letter claiming that Margaret Thatcher's monetarist policies would result in economic disaster. In America the battle was just as bitter. The Keynesians were seen as smug, prosperous, Ivy Leaguers who did not care that the policies they were advocating would ultimately result in inflation. Critics argued that by promoting a bigger role for government, they were also coloured with a pinkish political tinge. The monetarists, in contrast, came from outside the establishment. They fought a guerrilla campaign against the prevailing Keynesian orthodoxy, with their belief not only in sound money but also in free markets and small government. They were terrier-like, and none more so than Milton Friedman.

Friedman, born in Brooklyn in 1912 to poor, first-generation Jewish immigrant parents, nearly did not become an economist at all, lack of money threatening to cut short his studies. Fortunately he was able to persevere, and fortunately too, he found himself at the University of Chicago. The Chicago school of economics, like the Austrian school associated with important names such as Ludwig von Mises and Friedrich Hayek, to whom there is sadly not enough space in this book to do justice, kept the free market/sound money tradition going at a time when it was in danger of being snuffed out. Half the world was pursuing versions of Marxist economics, while the other half was, to free market thinkers, following a course that was nearly as dangerous, that of far-reaching government intervention. Through economists such as Henry Simons, Lloyd Mints, Frank Knight and Jacob Viner, Chicago in the 1930s and 1940s, stood as a bastion against the Keynesian thinking sweeping the world of economics.

Friedman, who was to later feature in his own television series on economics, providing a graphic demonstration of the way inflation is created by switching on a banknote printing press, made three key contributions. The first, in 1956, was his revival of Fisher's quantity theory of money. His paper, 'The Quantity Theory of Money: A Restatement', did more than dust off Fisher's work. He also addressed one of the fundamental Keynesian criticisms of monetarism, that there could never be a stable and predictable relationship between M, money, and P, prices, because the amount of money people wished to hold – the demand for money – was inherently unstable. Friedman agreed that money was only one of a number of assets that people wanted, the others being anything from stocks and shares through to cars, consumer durables and houses. He also developed, as noted earlier, the concept of 'permanent' income. The permanent income hypothesis was simply the idea that people have a notion of what their long-run, or permanent, income is. In other words, they look beyond temporary windfalls and shortfalls. Tied to this, said Friedman, they also have a clear idea of how much money they want to hold, for precautionary and other purposes, in relation to that permanent income. So what happens when the money supply increases? Everybody finds that they have more money, in relation to those other assets and their permanent income, than they want. Their response is to get rid of the money by buying, not only other financial assets (saving), but cars, washing machines, anything. An increase in the money supply stimulates spending. Part of that spending results in higher economic growth but much of it, he argued, would spill over into inflation. Inflation, he said famously, was 'always and everywhere' a monetary phenomenon, and the relationship between money and prices was as robust as any in science.

His second big contribution, with Anna Schwarz, was a massive exercise, *A Monetary History of the United States*, published in 1963. This not only demonstrated that the relationships he had postulated in his version of the quantity theory worked in practice (although others disputed that) but, more importantly, it provided a completely different take on America's Great Depression of 1929–33. It was, said Friedman and Schwarz, nothing to do with Keynes's liquidity trap, or a crisis in capitalism to which only public works programmes could provide the answer. Instead, there was a straightforward monetary explanation. The Federal Reserve, America's central bank, had become worried about the pace of economic expansion in 1928, when the roaring twenties were still roaring, and started to apply the monetary brakes. It applied them a little too hard and by the following year, when banks were failing across America as financial confidence ebbed, the money supply was dropping like a stone. The Great Depression was, said Friedman, testimony to the power of monetary policy. The economy 'fell because the Federal Reserve System forced or permitted a sharp reduction in the monetary base, because it failed to exercise the responsibilities assigned to it in the Federal Reserve Act to provide liquidity to the banking system'.

The natural rate

Finally, Friedman gave us a tool that economists and policy-makers use extensively, with varying success. The 'natural rate of unemployment' sounds like a very clinical concept, which is perhaps why it is more usually expressed these days as the much clumsier 'non-accelerating inflation rate of unemployment' (Nairu). Horrible expression, it just means the unemployment rate at which inflation is stable. Push unemployment too low, and upward pressures on wages – together with expectations of rising prices – will result in higher inflation. Allow unemployment to rise too high and the result should be falling inflation. It sounds more precise than it is. Economists waste a lot of time trying to work out what the Nairu is, only to find that in practice unemployment can fall below that level without triggering higher inflation. In the late 1990s unemployment in Britain and the United States dropped well below existing estimates of the Nairu. Anyway, back to the natural rate. In his presidential address to the American Economic Association in 1967, Friedman took on the Keynesian Phillips curve. The Phillips curve, which you may remember was invented at the London School of Economics by the same Bill Phillips who designed and built machines to display the workings of the economy, demonstrated the relationship between unemployment and wage inflation. When unemployment went up, inflation went down, and vice versa. For governments fine-tuning the economy through Keynesian demand management (small touches on the tiller by means of tax or public spending changes), the Phillips curve told them what to do. If inflation is too high, just apply the brakes by raising taxes and cutting spending – in other words create a bit of unemployment. If inflation is very low and unemployment high, then create a bit of growth, perhaps by boosting public spending. To Friedman this represented a fundamental misunderstanding of the way inflation worked, and he developed the natural rate to demonstrate why.

Let us say the natural rate of unemployment in the economy is 5 per cent of the workforce. It is at this level because, perhaps, there is always a certain amount of 'frictional' unemployment – people moving between jobs – but also because some people lack the necessary skills, and others are stuck in regions where there is little work available and it is difficult for them to move elsewhere. Now suppose a government is elected on a promise of halving unemployment. It tries to do so by expanding the economy, both through fiscal and monetary policy (increasing the money supply). Initially it works. Faced with greater demand firms take on even those workers whose skills are not quite right and expand output. They also raise prices, confident about doing so because they see demand in the economy as strong, not least because of all those extra people in jobs. Lower unemployment results in higher inflation. Perhaps the inflation rate goes up from 2 to 4 per cent. So far this is just the Phillips curve. But Friedman then examined the next round. What would happen if the government tried to keep unemployment below its natural rate by keeping its foot on the accelerator? Next time round, workers would remember the higher inflation of the previous episode and would want compensating for it in higher wages. Their 'expectations' have changed. They now expect inflation to be 2 per cent higher than its current rate, in other words 6 per cent, and so it goes on. The key point was that trying to keep unemployment below its natural rate did not just mean accepting a one-off rise in inflation. It meant accepting an accelerating rate of inflation (hence the Nairu). So is there nothing policymakers can do about unemployment, if its natural rate or Nairu happens to be high? Not at all. One of the big debates at present is how Europe can reduce its high Nairu, without accepting an accelerating inflation rate, by making its job markets more flexible.

The earliest and perhaps purest expression of the natural rate doctrine by a British politician was in 1976 when James Callaghan, the Labour Prime Minister, had reluctantly recognized that the old policies had run their course. In his speech to his 1976 party conference, written by his monetarist convert son-in-law Peter Jay, Callaghan said:

> We used to think that you could just spend your way out of recession, and increase employment, by cutting taxes and boosting government spending. I tell you in all candour that that option no longer exists, and in so far as it ever did exist, it worked by injecting inflation into the economy. And each time that happened, the average level of unemployment has risen. Higher inflation, followed by higher unemployment. That is the history of the last twenty years.

Lucas and the rationalists

Friedman's introduction of the natural rate of unemployment emphasized the role of expectations in influencing behaviour and the effectiveness of policy. Friedman's version of the Phillips curve is sometimes known as the 'expectations-augmented' Phillips curve. In the 1970s a group of American economists took this a stage further. Robert Lucas, Thomas Sargent and John Muth, particularly Lucas, gave us 'rational' expectations. Rational expectations was, like all great breakthroughs, very simple. The Lucas critique of conventional Keynesian econom- ics was that it assumed people were stupid. Take a typical situa- tion in British electoral politics. The governing party, seeking re-election, has a spring Budget ahead of a summer election. It cuts taxes and ensures interest rates are falling (not so easy now with an independent Bank of England). Voters feel good, hap- pily give their support, but a few months later, as night follows day, taxes and interest rates are going back up again. If voters are stupid that might happen over and over again. Rational expec- tations proposed that, just like laboratory rats or mice, we learn from our mistakes. If we get stung once, we won't go there again. This applied, of course, not just to pre-election economic policy but also to policy in general. Keynesian demand manage- ment worked because people responded to the initial economic stimulus, the tax cuts or extra public spending, by spending more themselves, blissfully unaware of the higher inflation that would follow. The Lucas critique said this would not happen. People would immediately look through to the higher inflation, and not respond to the inducements of policymakers. They would beware governments bearing gifts.

Are people rational in this way? It is hard to say. The mere fact that governments have persisted with election economics for very many years would suggest that it is possible to fool some of the people at least some of the time. There are plenty of examples where people continue doing things long after it appears to be rational. The boom in technology shares in the second half of the 1990s resulted in a peak for the Nasdaq (the US index of mainly technology stocks) of over 5,000 in March 2000. Within a year or so the index had plunged to less than a third of that peak. Well before shares had reached the peak Alan Greenspan, the Federal Reserve chairman, had warned of 'irrational' exuberance. There is another interesting idea attached to the behaviour of, for example, share markets. The 'efficient market hypothesis' says, in essence, that a market will settle at a level that efficiently reflects the current state of information available to investors. How can a market be efficient which is over 5,000 one year and 1,500 the next? The answer, which may not be entirely helpful to anybody wanting to determine in a scientific way whether stocks are cheap or dear, is that part of the information being used efficiently by investors at the peak was that there were plenty of suckers out there apparently willing to buy, whatever the price.

Anyway, back to rational expectations. The Lucas critique suggested that there was no point governments trying to prevent cyclical variations in the economy – boom and bust – because people and businesses would always, by operating rationally, be able to second-guess policy decisions. Lucas had another reason for rejecting such a policy approach. He is also a proponent of what is called 'real business cycle theory'. The Keynesians believed that the business cycle (the tendency of the economy to have periods of boom followed by slow growth or recession) was caused by variations in demand, in other words in investment and consumer demand. The real business cycle theorists argue, in contrast, that the cycle is due to variations in supply, to positive and negative economic shocks. In particular, periods of boom are caused by the discovery or spread of new technology – such as America's information and communications technology (ICT) boom of the 1990s – while recessions happen when the positive shocks have worn off and, for example, productivity (output per worker) growth is low. The traditional Keynesian solution of trying to prevent recession by increasing government spending is misplaced. Some would go so far as to claim that any kind of stabilization policy, for example the Bank of England cutting interest rates in a slowdown, is inappropriate. Booms and recessions are part of the natural order of things, they would argue, and trying to prevent them may do more harm than good. Few policymakers, it should be said, subscribe to this view.

Laffer and the supply-siders

Every era brings to the fore economists who seem particularly attuned to the political mood. In the 1980s when, under Ronald Reagan in America and Margaret Thatcher in Britain, there was an emphasis on tax cuts as a way to restore incentives and boost long-run growth, it was the supply-siders. A few years earlier

Arthur Laffer, then an economics professor at the University of California, was demonstrating to a writer from the *Wall Street Journal* how raising taxes could destroy the economy's productive potential. On a restaurant napkin he drew the Laffer curve. It showed that there are tax rates, zero and 100 per cent, when the government gets no revenue at all. When the tax rate is zero, it is self-evident that no revenue comes in. But none comes in either with a 100 per cent tax rate because there is no point anybody working. Between those two points, there will be a range of combinations of tax rates and revenue. As drawn by Laffer, tax revenue would rise in line with increases in tax rates up to a certain point but then revenue would fall, because high tax rates provide a disincentive for people to work. If the country was already beyond that point, it could even be the case that cutting tax rates would bring in extra revenue. The supply-siders, who included Paul Craig Roberts and Robert Mundell, provided intellectual support for tax cuts.

Supply-side economics goes beyond tax cuts, however, and it is no longer associated just with the American right and their bible, the *Wall Street Journal*. Supply-side economics embraces anything that raises the economy's long-run, or sustainable, growth rate. This might be tax cuts, or it might be increasing competition by breaking up cartels, attacking the restrictive practices of trade unions, improving the climate for business start-ups, or making it easier to hire and fire workers. Supply-side economics means taking action to enable the economy to achieve its potential, and increasing that potential.

American miscellany

America has produced many great economists in the post-war period. There is neither time nor space to mention them all. The great thing about economists in America is that they have had the time and the resources to take the subject into new areas. Gary Becker, who has applied economics to pretty well everything, was mentioned in an earlier chapter. James Tobin, who died in 2002, twenty-one years after winning the Nobel Prize, was another. His 'Tobin tax' – a tax on speculative foreign exchange transactions to be used to help the world's poor – became a totem for poverty pressure groups and anti-globalization protestors, even though, at the time of writing, it had not been taken up by policymakers. Tobin served in the US Navy in the Second World War, alongside Herman Wouk, who was later to write *The Caine Mutiny* and feature Tobin in it, thinly disguised as a character named Tobit. Tobin's work was wide-ranging. He demonstrated how financial markets fitted into a Keynesian economic framework with his research on portfolio selection. He showed how the characteristics of households affect their economic behaviour (this was called the 'Tobit analysis'). Most of all, he provided financial market analysts with a tool, called Tobin's 'q' – the relationship between a company's stock market valuation and its underlying net worth – for calculating whether a share, and the stock market as a whole, is overvalued or undervalued.

Another fascinating branch of economic theory developed by American economists, particularly James Buchanan and Gordon Tullock, is public choice theory. Public choice theory applies economic principles to the behaviour of voters, political leaders and bureaucrats. The behaviour of bureaucrats, for example, is governed by self-interest not a desire to selflessly serve the community. So they are driven by salary, position and the perks of office, reputation and power. Elected politicians, meanwhile, are driven by the desire to be re-elected but are prey to powerful interest groups. Voters, who should check and balance the behaviour of politicians, are not particularly efficient at doing so. Public choice theory suggests that, unless controlled, government will tend to grow bigger and bigger. Its proponents argue for such controls. Tax rises, for example, should be permitted only if two-thirds or three-quarters of the legislature approve, and bureaucrats should be allowed to hold office only for a limited time.

*
**

It is time to move on. I have not touched on some of the recent debates among American economists, such as whether there was a 'new' economy of genuinely stronger productivity growth in the 1990s. Some, such as Robert Gordon, argued that there was an improvement in productivity but that it was confined to the IT sector. Others preferred to believe that there was an economy-wide improvement.

I should also provide the denouement to that long battle between the monetarists and the Keynesians. To talk of consensus and economics in the same sentence may be stretching things but it is fair to say that there has been a coming together between the Keynesians and the monetarists. The Keynesians accept that money matters, as does the supply-side. The monetarists, or most of them, concede that there is more to running the economy than simply setting targets for the money supply and sticking to them. Pragmatism is in vogue.

13

Arguing over coffee

All good meals, and all books, must come to an end. It would be wrong, however, to disappear into the night without a chat, perhaps even a little debate. Economists argue all the time. The subject advances, or sometimes goes back a little, by means of constructive engagement. To some, economists disagree a little too much. Churchill famously said that if you had two economists in a room you were guaranteed two different points of view, 'and three if one of them is Mr Keynes'. That may be a little too harsh. Where would we be without controversy? The comforting thing about economics, indeed, is that it is often possible for both sides to be right. With this in mind, let us have a look at some long-standing controversies.

Why are some countries richer than others?
In the end, there are perhaps only two economic questions that

matter – how much wealth is created and how it is distributed between people and countries. Since Adam Smith's day the world has created wealth at an exponential rate. Its distribution has, however, become more uneven as time has gone on. The disparities in income and wealth between the world's rich and poor are striking. Estimates published in the *Economic Journal* in 2002 by Branko Milanovic of the World Bank showed that the richest 1 per cent of the world's population, approximately 60 million people, received as much income as the poorest 57 per cent, 3.4 billion. David Landes, the economic historian, estimates that the income gap between one of the richest countries, Switzerland, and one of the poorest, Mozambique, is 400 to one. Prior to the industrial revolution of the middle of the eighteenth century, he suggests, the biggest such gap would be about five to one. The richest fifth of the world's population receives 86 per cent of global income and 1.2 billion people, 20 per cent of the world's population, exist on less than a dollar a day, with another 2 billion officially categorized as 'in poverty'. Rich countries spawn rich companies. Large, multinational firms account for one-third of world gross domestic product and two-thirds of world trade.

Why such disparities? There are three broad explanations. The first is the 'late developer' thesis. Political correctness requires that we call poor countries developing countries even when some of them are not developing at all. On this view, prosperity and success eventually come to everybody but for some it takes longer than others. African countries, for example, have a level of income per head about the same as that of Europe two centuries ago. Perhaps in two centuries they may be only a hundred years behind Europe, and thus well above present European living standards. It is a big perhaps. It is true that changes have taken place in the global economic rankings. As the cradle of the industrial revolution Britain had first mover advantage – by starting first she managed to stay ahead of the pack – and reigned supreme for a hundred years or so after it. The writing was on the wall, however, as early as the Great Exhibition of 1851, when people began to notice the superiority of the products being exhibited by German companies. Britain was caught and surpassed, not just by other European economies, but also more particularly by America. Japan, an economy closed to the outside world until late in the nineteenth century, was another to come through rapidly, both before and even more impressively after the devastation of the Second World War. China could have had an industrial revolution at the time of the European renaissance but chose a different path. Now, say some, China will be the most powerful economy of the twenty-first century, although there are serious reasons to question this, most notably whether it has the appropriate economic structure for sustained growth.

The fact that countries have changed position in the rankings does not, however, offer comfort. Anti-globalization critics would argue that the rich countries and their corporations have organized things in such a way that they have effectively kicked the ladder away. Poor countries, in other words, are there to exploit, not to provide with a helping-hand. This criticism cannot be dismissed out of hand, and certainly richer countries have tended to control the rules of global trade and have done so in a way that excludes the products of poor countries. That, we hope, is changing. As for corporations, their main interest is in creating new markets of prosperous customers, not in preserving poverty. We must look for another explanation for persistent poverty.

The second explanation has to do with location. The eminent Canadian-born (but American-adopted) economist J. K. Galbraith noted years ago that if you were to mark a line around the globe a thousand miles either side of the equator there would be no developed, that is rich, countries there. Poor countries tend to be in tropical and semi-tropical zones. There, disease tends to be rife, including traditional diseases such as malaria and modern ones such as AIDS, life expectancy low. Agriculture is more difficult and less productive, so producing a relatively small amount of food absorbs a great deal of labour. Many poor countries, particularly those in Africa, are poorly placed geographically to benefit from trade. Landlocked countries, in particular, struggle, most notably if they are in dispute with the neighbours they need to traverse to get to the seas. A study by Jeffrey Sachs and others put down Africa's economic failure to climate, disease, geography and poor policies. Non-tropical South Africa is about five times as wealthy, per capita, as tropical Africa, and not just because of gold and diamonds.

The third explanation, put forward by David Landes in his fine book *The Wealth and Poverty of Nations*, is that it all comes down to culture. Landes's title deliberately echoes Adam Smith's *Wealth of Nations*. Smith, you will recall, explained the route to prosperity through the division of labour. Organization was the key to harnessing and advancing the powerful forces of industrialization. Britain, as the first modern industrial country, was ideally placed to take advantage of it. There was a powerful desire for economic advancement, a willingness to embrace new technology, an already well-developed capital market (the City), a rule of law and a respect for property rights. Other countries, often with similar societies – Germany, America, Australia, and others – either possessed or were able to emulate this work ethic.

Whether that work ethic was Protestant in origin can be debated, but that would certainly not explain Japan's success. In other parts of the world, however, religion, whether it is Roman Catholicism or Islam, appears to have inhibited economic development. 'If we learn anything from the history of economic development it is that culture makes all the difference,' Landes writes.

Witness the enterprise of expatriate communities – the Chinese in East and Southeast Asia, Indians in East Africa, Lebanese in West Africa, Jews and Calvinists throughout much of Europe, and on and on. Yet culture, in the sense of the inner values and attitudes that guide a population, frightens scholars. It has a sulphuric odour of race and inheritance, an air of immutability.

His message should be an optimistic one. Cultures can change, adapt. Many countries have a tradition of enterprise even if their most entrepreneurial people tend to express themselves elsewhere. In a sense most development programmes follow his line

of thinking. The tools of development are as much the establishment of the rule of law, of property rights, of efficient government, as the granting of foreign aid. Lord Bauer, the
distinguished British economist who died in 2002, pointed out
that over decades indiscriminate aid did poor countries more
harm than good. Douglass North, the American economic historian and joint winner of the Nobel Prize for economics in
1993, has studied the role of institutions in economic development. According to him: 'Institutions provide the basic structure
by which human beings throughout history have created order
and attempted to reduce uncertainty in exchange.' The inability
to enter into binding contracts and the prevalence of bribery and
corruption hold back development both in the poor countries
and in the former socialist states. Get the institutions right and
you have a chance. And yet the message is also a depressing one.
People have known for years that there are cultural barriers to
economic development. There are good examples of where
those barriers have been lowered but plenty of others where
those advocating such reforms have been knocking their heads
against a brick wall, not least because the fruits of even small-
scale development have gone to corrupt rulers, rather than the
general population. The poor have stayed poor, and may remain
so.

Is globalization a bad thing?

Closely related to the existence of huge inequalities between
countries is the role of globalization. It is a term much bandied
around, but what does it mean? According to a definition used

by Britain's Department for International Development (DfID), which recently produced a white paper on the subject, globalization is

the growing interdependence and interconnectedness of the modern world through increased flows of goods, services, capital, people and information. The process is driven by technological advances and reductions in the costs of international transactions, which speed technology and ideas, raise the share of trade in world production and increase the mobility of capital.

It is not, in other words, just Coca Colonization – the dominance of the world by a few large companies and brands – although the global corporation is clearly an aspect of it. It is the movement of vast sums of money around the international financial system, the fact that the toy in your child's Christmas stocking was probably made in China. It is the breakdown of barriers. It is the fact that, more than ever, no country is an island unto itself in economic terms. The old chaos theory cliché, that a butterfly flapping its wings in the Amazon jungle could cause a hurricane thousands of miles away, has its parallels in our globalized world. To take an obvious example, a computer hacker in Manila who invents the 'I love you' virus can cause panic in offices thousands of miles away.

Beginning at the World Trade Organization ministerial meeting in Seattle in November 1999, and at most gatherings of political and business leaders since, anti-globalization protestors, often using violent methods, have been out in force. Whether you agree with it and its methods or not, the campaign has been a considerable success in making politicians, businessmen and economists think. It has high-profile supporters. 'For millions of people globalization has not worked,' wrote Joseph Stiglitz, former chief economist at the World Bank, in his 2002 book *Globalization and Its Critics*. 'Many have actually been made worse off, as they have seen their jobs destroyed and their lives become more insecure. They have felt increasingly powerless against forces beyond their control. They have seen their democracies undermined, their cultures eroded.' The new world trade round launched in Qatar in November 2001 was called the 'Doha development agenda', an explicit recognition that the future opening-up of world trade must be geared towards the needs of poor countries.

Economists, as a rule, have little difficulty in agreeing that free trade is highly beneficial. A crucial element in post-1945 global prosperity, out of the ashes of the protectionism of the inter-war years, has been trade liberalization – the removal of barriers to trade, both formal and informal, under the auspices of first the General Agreement on Tariffs and Trade (GATT) and then the World Trade Organization. Free trade has had a powerful effect. Countries have become more open and have mainly benefited hugely from it. World trade growth has, over time, averaged two or three times the rate of growth of national output. Developing countries that have adopted free trade rules have experienced growth rates averaging 4.5 per cent a year over the past three decades, compared with 0.7 per cent for the limited number of closed economies.

So what is the debate? It is that free trade, far from being of mutual benefit, has been a means of exploiting the world's poor. According to Oxfam, in an April 2002 report entitled *Rigged Rules and Double Standards*, for every $100 generated by world exports, only $3 goes to poor countries; and for every dollar given to developing countries in aid, $2 is lost because of unfair trade rules which are costing them $100 billion a year. Tariffs and taxes on imports levied by rich countries are four times as high when the imports are from poor countries as from other industrial countries. Perhaps the worst examples of where trade acts against the interests of poor countries are in agriculture, where rich countries spend $1 billion a day on farm subsidies, exporting surpluses on world markets in a way that drives down prices for farmers in developing countries. None of this suggests that the world should abandon the quest for free trade, or that poor countries would be better off by opting out of the global system. What it does say is that a meaningful drive for free trade would target the cosy little deals that enable rich countries to scratch each others' backs, and which protect their domestic industries and farmers. During 2002 George W. Bush, supposedly a free trader, signed into law tariff barriers against steel imports, to protect America's bloated and inefficient producers.

One of the paradoxes about free trade is that creation of free trade areas, such as the European Union's single market or the North American Free Trade Agreement involving the United States, Mexico and Canada, can actually be damaging to free trade, if the existence of these 'preferential trading agreements' have the effect of excluding other countries. According to

Jagdish Bhagwati, one of the world's leading experts on trade, in his book *Free Trade Today*:

> *We are thus reproducing in the world trading system, in the name of free trade but through free trade areas that spread discrimination against producers in non-member countries, the chaos that was created in the 1930s through similar uncoordinated pursuit of protectionism that discriminated in favour of domestic producers. In both cases, the preferred solution would have been non-discriminatory pursuit of freer trade.*

Are high taxes good or bad for you?

One of the most enduring debates in economics is over the level of tax and government spending, and whether high taxes depress economic growth. In the previous chapter we encountered the American supply-siders, and the view that after a point high taxation not only did economic damage but was counter-productive in terms of its main purpose, that of raising revenue. It was an article of faith when the Conservatives were in power in the 1980s that lowering taxes on income boosted incentives (mainly for the better-off) and led to stronger sustained growth, for supply-side reasons. Tony Blair's Labour government explicitly moved away from this line of thinking in the April 2002 Budget, raising National Insurance contributions, a tax on income, for all, for the purposes of boosting public spending. On average across the industrial countries, government spending has increased from about 11 per cent of gross domestic product in 1870, when it was mainly concentrated on military expenditure, to just under 45 per cent now, when it covers an array of public services, as well as the welfare state. In relatively recent history in Britain, the overwhelming majority of working people paid no income tax. Now the vast majority do so.

Yet the rise and rise of government spending, and therefore taxation, has been associated with more prosperity, not less. Where has the damage occurred, when real disposable incomes, after allowing for inflation and tax, have increased to record levels in spite of a rise in the government's share of GDP? The puzzle becomes even greater when we look at comparisons between countries. At the time of writing both America and Japan have levels of tax of about 30 per cent of GDP. America is a highly successful and dynamic economy while Japan, during the 1990s, appeared to have entered a state of permanent depression. One of the most successful economies in Europe, Finland, has government spending and tax of just under 50 per cent of GDP while another, Ireland, has about 35 per cent. On the face of it, there is no relationship between the level of tax and public spending and economic performance. How would an economist go about trying to solve this puzzle?

The answer is firstly to deconstruct some of the data. Yes, prosperity has risen strongly during a period in which the size of government has increased. It may be, however, that it would have risen a lot more if tax and public spending had remained lower, as some studies have shown. The second point is to recognize that the size of government is not the only factor at work at any time. If we take the Japan–America comparison, for example, one argument would be that Japan's low tax advantage in the 1990s was swamped by other factors, most notably the prolonged effects of the abrupt ending of a huge speculative boom (the 'bubble' economy) and an ageing population. Not only that, but the response of the Japanese government to the difficulties of the 1990s was to increase public spending sharply, which could have added to the problem. More fundamentally, at the root of the tax-and-spending question is the motto of this book, there being no such thing as a free lunch. There is a cost to raising tax, for it means, in the case of individuals, that they will tend to have less incentive to work and less money to spend. Against this have to be set the benefits of government spending. A government that spends wisely and efficiently on health, education and other public services, with the full support of taxpayers, may do so in a way that not only offsets the economic costs incurred in taxation but also sometimes exceeds them. There is a net benefit, in other words, from raising taxes to increase government spending. Thus countries that spend taxpayers' money efficiently can prosper with higher taxes than others. The settled societies of the Scandinavian countries, which at one stage increased government spending to 60 per cent of GDP, appeared to be examples of this. Appropriately enough it was a Swedish economist, Knut Wicksell, who gave us the notion of the 'Wicksellian equilibrium', the level of tax and government spending that most closely reflected society's preferences.

All this still leaves some economists uneasy. Surely there must be some kind of rule that can be laid down about optimal size of government, the level of taxation, even if there will always be exceptions to that rule. In general, studies show that government spending is quite efficient when it starts from a low level and, for example, introduces universal education, healthcare and a pension safety net. These things, particularly better education and health, contribute to economic growth. A major study by Vito Tanzi and Ludger Schuknecht, *Public Spending in the 20th Century: A Global Perspective*, as well as work by Robert Barro, conclude that the gains between 1870, when public spending in industrial countries averaged 11 per cent of GDP, and 1960, by which time it was nearly 30 per cent, were well worth having for those reasons. Beyond that, however, any gains are questionable. 'We have argued that most of the important social and economic gains can be achieved with a drastically lower level of public spending than prevails today,' Tanzi and Schuknecht wrote. 'Perhaps, the level of public spending does not need to be much higher than 30 per cent of GDP to achieve most of the important social and economic objectives that justify government interventions. However, this would require radical reforms, a well-working private market, and an efficient regulatory role for government.'

David Smith, a namesake of mine who works for the City firm Williams de Broë, has tried to calculate the effects on economic growth from boosting government spending's share beyond 1960 levels. His work suggests that in all cases there has been a negative impact, although the impact varies. In America, where the spending boost has been smallest, growth has suffered an average 0.8 per cent a year loss. In Britain, it is 1.1 per cent. But in Sweden, where the size of government grew most rapidly, the effect was to depress growth by a huge 3.7 per cent a year. At a time when the Labour government in Britain has embarked on a big increase in government spending, it is worth reminding ourselves that some things do not come free.

Is the euro a good idea?

There will be those who argue that taxation and government spending raise questions beyond economics, questions of philosophy and the freedom of the individual. And there are plenty of people who say that the European single currency raises profound questions of politics and sovereignty. If Britain were to throw in her lot with Europe by joining the euro – hot topic at the time of writing – some would say it would be the equivalent of signing up to a European super state. Whether that is true or not, it remains the case that economics should play a central role in any decision on joining the euro, as explicitly recognized by Tony Blair's government. It set five *economic* tests for entry – whether it would be good for jobs, the City and investment, and whether Britain was sufficiently converged with Europe, as well as being flexible enough, to make a success of membership.

The question of euro entry lends itself perfectly to cost–benefit analysis, to assessing the arguments on either side. I say perfectly, but there will always be room for dispute among economists about the extent of those costs and benefits. There is, too, the matter of attributing risk. Suppose, as with any decision, there is the potential for a series of small gains but on the other side, a risk, perhaps a small one, of complete disaster. Correctly assessing the disaster risk is plainly pivotal to making the right decision. Anyway, what are the costs and benefits of the euro,

229

and in particular of UK entry? Let me start with the benefits:

▶ Joining the euro means certainty and stability for business, particularly exporters. In Britain, where firms have had to cope over the years with a highly volatile exchange rate, this could be a significant plus. Firms could plan long-term strategies for export markets on the basis of currency certainty, and invest accordingly.

▶ It could lead to an increase in trade. Europe's single market, free movement of goods, services, capital and people, officially commenced at the end of 1992, although it has yet to be completed in many of these areas. One argument is that having different currencies is itself a significant barrier to trade and until all fifteen (at the time of writing) EU members have adopted it Europe can never be a true single market, on the scale of, say, America. A single currency, in other words, is needed for a single market.

▶ It lowers and in many cases removes transaction costs. Everybody knows the story, perhaps apocryphal, of somebody who starts in Dover with £100, changing into local currency each time he visits a different EU country (this is a pre-euro story). By the time he gets back the £100 has gone, not because it has been spent but because each time commission has had to be paid for changing the cash. As I said, this is a pre-euro story. Even so, UK individuals and companies dealing with Europe still have to go through the hassle and expense of changing currency. These costs are not high — removing them was calculated by the European

Commission to be worth 0.3 to 0.4 per cent of EU GDP annually – but they are not negligible either.

▶ Interest rates are lower in the euro area, 'euroland'. For a long time, not least when interest rates of 10 or 12 per cent or higher were common in Britain, one of the most powerful attractions of the euro (which then was still a twinkle in the eye of European politicians) was that it would offer significantly lower interest rates. Britain, in a sense, could buy into Germany's low-inflation credibility. Economists would say that Britain's interest rates were high for a reason, notably because the economy was prone to high inflation, but to the extent that rates were high because of sterling's recurrent vulnerability, there was a point. Joining the euro provided a huge boom for some countries. Italy, for example, found that it could fund its government debt at significantly lower interest rates, removing its budget deficit problem at a stroke. For Britain the argument has diminished as interest rates have come down, although it is still the case that short-term rates – those set by the Bank of England and European Central Bank respectively – tend to be slightly lower in Europe.

▶ The euro also creates price transparency. For years it has been an observable fact that prices across a range of products are higher in Britain than in other countries, including those in the rest of the EU. In some cases price differentials have narrowed, for example in cars, as result of action by the European Commission and the domestic competition authorities. But in many cases significant differences persist, and 'rip-off Britain' remains a reality. When everything is priced in euros, it is argued, such differentials will not only become more transparent than they are now but they will also be difficult to sustain. The euro, after the changeover period, will deliver lower prices for consumers (when the twelve members of euroland switched to notes and coins in early 2002 there were many examples of prices being rounded higher).

Some of these advantages can be questioned. Yes, the euro would remove currency instability within Europe, which is where nearly 60 per cent of Britain's visible exports (goods) go, but under 50 per cent of total trade. It would, however, do nothing about instability with regard, say, to the dollar. The single market, as noted, needs a lot more than a single currency to complete it. Transaction costs are small, and arguably getting smaller in an era of electronic money. The interest rate gains are not significant any more. As for price transparency, as long as there are tax differences between EU members, and as long as product differences persist (something manufacturers are keen to preserve), it may not happen.

There is a bigger argument against the euro, however, and it has to do with what is sometimes called, in shorthand, the 'one size fits all' problem. Countries in the euro have to adopt the same exchange rate. A single currency means just that. No longer can France alter its exchange rate vis-à-vis Germany, or any of the other euro member countries. A euro is a euro, the currency shared by people from Berlin to Barcelona, Lisbon to

Leipzig. They also, however, have to live with the same interest rate, set by the European Central Bank. Each country, admittedly, has a voting representative on the ECB's rate-setting council but each, too, is implicitly accepting that they can live with the interest rate set by others. The easiest kind of monetary union would be between two identical countries, each with similar industries and similar vulnerability to economic shocks. If oil prices go up, or the price of cotton goes down, they are affected in the same way. Sharing a currency and an interest rate poses no dangers, as long as they started with roughly the same economic performance. There would clearly be trouble if, at the outset, one country had zero inflation, the other a 100 per cent rate. This was why, when the decision was taken to proceed with the euro at Maastricht in 1991, conditions, or criteria, were set down, requiring countries wishing to take part to have broadly similar inflation, long-term interest rates, budget deficits and debt. The criteria, it should be said, were not always observed to the letter, particularly in the case of budget deficits and debt. Suppose, though, that, unlike our two similar countries, euro participants are very different, which comes closer to reflecting reality. The members of the EU differ in size, in industrial structure, in dependence on oil, in the proportion of GDP they export to non-EU countries. As individual countries with their own central banks, they could compensate when such differences began to tell by adjusting interest rates. In euroland that is not possible. Thus a standard piece of economics is the theory of optimal currency areas, most associated with Robert Mundell, the

Canadian-born Nobel Prize-winning economist.

An optimal currency area requires either all participants to be not only closely interlinked through trade, but also broadly similar in structure. A single currency area that consisted of two economies, one whose sole product was wheat, the other cars, would be unlikely to work. A slump in world wheat prices would hurt one badly while leaving the other unaffected. Looked at another way, countries have to have the ability to respond to economic shocks, an example of which might be a sharp rise in world oil prices. There are three conditions for an optimal currency area. The first is 'geographical mobility' of labour. If people are made unemployed in one part of the euro area, they have to be willing to move to where the jobs are. The second requirement, either in tandem with or instead of geographical mobility, is wage flexibility. Suppose there is a shock that is threatening big job losses in one region. They have to be prepared to accept a cut in wages to persuade the employer not to pull out. The third requirement is a large enough central budget, so that fiscal policy can be used to provide help where monetary policy – which is set for the whole area – cannot. In America's single currency (dollar) area, the federal budget works in precisely this way. When there is a downturn in, say, California, Washington can provide direct help, not least through larger assistance payments. At the same time a phenomenon known by economists as the 'automatic stabilizers' operates. California, during its downturn, pays fewer taxes into the federal budget, helping the state get through its difficulty. Is Europe an optimal currency area? Prior to the launch of the euro some economists believed that a small group of countries at the heart of Europe – France, Germany, Belgium, Luxembourg and the Netherlands – fitted that description. Few believed that it was true for the eleven who made it to the starting-gate (Austria, Finland, Ireland, Italy, Portugal and Spain joined too), or the twelve (Greece quickly became a member) euroland consists of at the time of writing. Even the smallest of these groups, lacking sufficient geographical mobility of labour and wage flexibility, did not satisfy pure optimal currency area requirements. The EU as a whole, with a tiny central budget of just 1.27 per cent of GDP, is well below the 25 per cent of GDP level generally reckoned to be needed to provide a proper offset to monetary policy.

The story does not end there. Mundell, curiously, became an advocate of the euro because, equally curiously, he decided that there were never any optimal currency areas in real life, but that it was worth pressing ahead with monetary unions anyway. He argued, in fact, for a global single currency backed by gold. There is also a line of argument that, whether the starting-point is optimal or not, once inside a single currency countries will adjust and make it work. Whether that adjustment is at the cost of high unemployment, which is the natural consequence of forcing countries into an inappropriate monetary union, is the big worry.

For Britain, there is another consideration. Previous monetary arrangements between Britain and Europe have ended in disaster. In 1972 sterling stayed in the 'snake', a forerunner of the European Monetary System (EMS), for just six weeks. Between 1990 and 1992 Britain spent twenty-three agonizing months inside the exchange rate mechanism of the EMS, before the humiliating exit on 16 September 1992. In the past, Britain approached Europe in the position of supplicant, usually to obtain some much-needed support for the beleaguered pound or to acquire by association some of Germany's anti-inflation credibility. With the Bank of England independent, under arrangements that many consider superior to those of the ECB, and with Britain's recent economic performance having been better than the rest of the EU (in inflation, unemployment and growth), the balance has shifted. That does not mean everything in the garden is rosy. Productivity is significantly higher in France and Germany than in the UK, 40 and 20 per cent respectively, despite the government's efforts to close the gap. Europeans also look askance at the poor quality of Britain's transport infrastructure and public services. Improved UK economic performance, at the time of writing, does not mean that Britain should never join the euro but it does mean that the risks of losing something are greater. If the motto was 'if it ain't broke don't fix it', most economists would currently argue against membership. Whether that will be true for the longer term remains to be seen. Economists should also have a little humility in this debate. While they were given the role of assessing the Chancellor of the Exchequer's five economic tests for UK euro entry – whether the economy is sufficiently converged with Europe and also flexible, and whether entry would be good for jobs, investment and the City – nobody pretends economics has all the answers, particularly on the politics of the euro.

Does economics make you happy?

This may seem like an odd question, particularly when the subject has been known on and off since the nineteenth century as the dismal science, and when you do not have to look too hard to find some pretty gloomy economists. The economics of happiness is, however, one of the subject's growth areas. 'The extent to which people are happy or unhappy is an essential quality of the economy and society,' write Bruno Frey and Alois Stutzer in their book *Happiness and Economics*. 'The state of the economy strongly affects people's happiness.' How do you measure something as subjective as happiness? Mainly through surveys that ask people how satisfied they are with life, or with their job. One difficulty, of course, is that people's expectations change. Consumers come to expect product improvements, employees better working conditions. It is hard to compare two very different situations, to transform an individual's condition. A Victorian factory worker teleported to a modern industrial plant would think he had arrived in heaven. So would a Model T driver handed the keys of a modern car. However, most improvements are incremental. Whether people are happy or not depends on whether those improvements exceed, keep pace with, or fall behind the rise in expectations. This also applies to areas of public service delivery such as the National Health Service, as successive British governments have discovered.

So what do we know about happiness? Andrew Oswald and Jonathan Gardner of Warwick University are among the economists who have researched extensively in this field. Their work on job satisfaction suggests that it declined during the

1990s, particularly among women and public sector workers. Of more interest, perhaps, is that the happiest workers in Britain are those with no educational qualifications (and lower job expectations), while the least satisfied are those with a degree. This may suggest that many people are over-qualified for their jobs, particularly those with degrees. People with postgraduate degrees, interestingly, are happier at work than graduates. Women tend to be happier at work than men. People in non-profit organizations have the most job satisfaction, probably because they feel they are doing good, followed by public sector workers, then those in the private sector. By age, the happiest workers are those in their sixties, with retirement just around the corner, the least happy are in their twenties. Oswald, along with David Blanchflower of Dartmouth College in America, also compared job satisfaction across nations. They found, in a survey of twenty-seven countries, Britain came seventeenth in terms of workers being satisfied with their lot at work. Denmark topped the rankings, while Cyprus, Israel, the Netherlands, the Philippines, Spain, Switzerland, the United States and even Russia had higher levels of job satisfaction than Britain.

Does money buy you happiness? Oswald and Gardner tested this by looking at the psychological health and happiness of a randomly chosen sample of 9,000 people. Some of those in the sample had been lucky enough to receive financial windfalls, such as lottery or football pools wins, or unexpected inheritances. On the basis of this information they were able to calculate the impact of money on happiness. A windfall of £50,000, or around $75,000, was sufficient to give people a significant lift in terms of happiness. But how much did it need to make a really miserable person happy? According to the study, a windfall of £1 million (about $1.5 million) was required to do this, to 'move someone from close to the bottom of a happiness frequency distribution to close to the top'. Does happiness bought by extra money last? Probably not. Further study is needed but intuitively it seems that windfall effects wear off over time. In addition, the effect of money can be relative. The same amount of wealth could make you feel as rich as Croesus in most parts of the world but a relative pauper in Monte Carlo or the Bahamas. Three Swedish economists, Olof Johansson-Stenman, Fredrik Carlsson and Dinky Daruvala, found in 2002 that people's happiness depended not just on absolute income, but also on their relative position in the income ladder. Not only that, but when a sample of people was surveyed using a series of scenario-based questions – they were asked to choose between two imaginary future societies – most expressed a preference for a more equitable distribution of income, largely because of the fear that they would end up at the bottom of the heap in an unequal society. Lots of conflicting factors come into the equation. People are competitive, driven by a desire to 'keep up with the Joneses', and their tastes and desires are conditioned by what others are doing. As Marx put it: 'A house may be large or small; as long as the neighbouring houses are likewise small, it satisfies all the social requirements for a residence. But let there arise next to the little house a palace, and the little house shrinks to a hut.'

Are we getting better off?

The economics of happiness is closely tied to another question, that of economic progress. When John Major was Prime Minister of Britain he made what to many seemed like a rash promise – that of doubling living standards over twenty-five years. Actually it was a rather safe pledge, on two counts. The first was that by the time anybody was able to check, Major would be long gone from politics (he soon was anyway). The second was that he was describing, more or less, what was already happening. The power of compound numbers is a wonderful thing. Economic growth of a shade over 2.5 per cent a year will produce a doubling of living standards every twenty-five years, just as economic growth of 4 per cent annually would produce it in fifteen years. Whether a doubling of gross domestic product per head, after allowing for inflation, is the same as a doubling of living standards is a matter of some debate. Many people would argue that while they are materially better off, the downsides of modern life – crime, congestion, stress, even declining moral standards – mean that GDP per capita is a poor measure of progress. Some economists favour other measures, which try to take into account other factors. The United Nations' human development index, which is particularly useful for measuring progress in poorer countries, takes into account factors such as life expectancy and educational provision.

The fact is that, in the absence of recessions, which tend to be short-lived, we do become better off each year. Harold Macmillan, one of Major's Tory predecessors, became associated with the phrase 'You've never had it so good', when he said in 1957:

'Let us be frank about it: most of our people have never had it so good.' Few Prime Ministers, in fact, would have been unable to make that boast. Living standards tend to improve, but at what rate? The answer to this, fairly obviously, is that it depends on circumstances. Nick Crafts, an economic history professor at the London School of Economics and a noted expert on long-term growth trends, has tracked Britain's growth rate, on a per capita basis, back to the nineteenth century. Dividing the period into four, 1870–1913, 1913–50, 1950–73 and 1973 until the end of the century, the results show rising GDP per capita in all four periods, but at different rates. In the first period, 1870–1913 (which included the so-called great depression of the late nineteenth century), GDP per capita rose by an average of 1 per cent a year. The second period, 1913–50, included two world wars and the more familiar Great Depression, and growth did well to average 0.9 per cent a year. The period 1950–73, known by economic historians as the 'golden age' of healthy growth, low inflation and full employment, saw GDP per capita rise by 2.4 per cent a year (Major was clearly thinking of a new golden age), while from 1973 onwards, as the economy hit oil crises, financial market instability, regular recessions and generally greater turbulence, growth slipped to 1.8 per cent a year.

More interesting than these bald figures is what was happening elsewhere. In the earliest period Britain's 1 per cent growth rate was by no means high, but it was in the same broad area as that of other countries. Already, however, with American per capita GDP rising by 1.8 per cent a year in the 1870–1913 period, the writing was on the wall. Again, in the period 1913–50, Britain held her own in comparison with other European countries but was well behind America's 1.6 per cent growth rate (think of the power of compound numbers). It was in the golden age, however, that a gap really opened up. Britain's 2.4 per cent growth rate over the 1950–73 period sounds respectable, and in fact matched that of America, but it was well behind France, 4 per cent, Germany and Italy, each 5 per cent, and Japan, 8 per cent. Crafts's contention is that over the past twenty years or so Britain has stopped the rot of relative economic decline, largely because of the policies adopted by the Thatcher government, many of which Labour retained when it took office in 1997. There have, of course, been countries with more rapid growth rates during this period, notably the Asian 'tiger' economies, at least up until the 1997–8 Asian crisis. There is no sign yet, though, that on a long view the British economy is performing better than that of competitors.

What causes economic growth?

Economies grow, and so do living standards, but why? Adam Smith gave us one important route – the gains from trade and from the division of labour mean that productivity, output per worker, increases from one year to the next. Karl Marx gave us another clue in his observation that all capitalists are interested in is investing, accumulating capital. A rise in the amount of capital equipment per worker will also tend to be associated with rising output per worker. Growth theory is an entire branch of economics in its own right. One interesting but difficult exercise is to try to account for economic growth by splitting it into its component parts. Angus Maddison, a specialist in this so-called 'growth accounting', has produced results that suggest investment other than in housing is the most important source of growth, with significant contributions also made by rising educational standards, trade and, for most countries, a 'catch-up' effect as they adopt the technology or methods used by countries with higher productivity levels.

Extra investment, the main source of growth, does not always flow smoothly. It is subject to – indeed is one of the primary causes of – the business cycle. It is also subject to more pronounced fluctuations, as new technologies become available. When people spoke of the 'new economy' of the ICT revolution of the 1990s, they were following a long tradition. There have been many 'new' economies over the ages, from the transformation of the cotton industry by the spinning jenny of James Hargreaves, Thomas Arkwright's water frame and Samuel Crompton's mule. Steam, canals, railways, electricity, radio in the 1920s and television in the 1950s – all have provided spurts of large-scale investment activity and an apparent move up to a new and higher plane of economic growth. In each case, the initial effect is to produce a sharp rise in productivity in the sector concerned, whether it is transport (canals and railways), energy production (electricity), media or ICT. Then, as this increase in productivity is passed on, falling prices lead to a boom in investment. There is also, typically, a restructuring of the economy around the new technology.

Why, if we have had all these 'new' economies over the decades, has productivity not grown even faster over time? To an extent, the story of the twentieth century, and in particular its second half, was about not just the invention of new technology but also the realization of its potential. There is also a sense, however, in which maintaining economic growth requires these bouts of what the Austrian economist Joseph Schumpeter called 'creative destruction'. He saw capitalist economies leading to episodes that 'incessantly revolutionise the economic structure from within, incessantly destroying the old one, incessantly creating a new one'. Put another way, when the effects of a technological revolution wear off, it is time for another one, otherwise growth will slow. Fortunately, capitalism has been reasonably good at coming up with periodic breakthroughs. There is one other lesson from 'new' economies, both ancient and modern. It is that in each case there is usually a stock market boom that anticipates the mass application of the new technology. The railway mania in Britain in the 1840s, when the shares of railway firms soared to sky-high levels before crashing back down to earth, was very similar in character to the Nasdaq boom of the 1990s. The lesson, in all cases, is that while some lucky investors do well, many have their fingers burned, both by the ups and downs of the share prices of even the successful innovating firms, and because there is inevitably a winnowing out process as the majority fall by the wayside. For every Microsoft that makes it, there are thousands of others that do not. New technology usually helps the economy more than it does the bank balances of investors.

Why do we need low inflation?

This is the kind of question you do not ask in the company of central bankers. It is also less commonly asked than it used to be in general conversation but you still hear it from time to time. When the Bank of England's monetary policy committee meets to set interest rates each month, there is often a trade union leader or Labour MP on hand to question its 'anti-inflation obsession', even though the government, not the Bank itself, sets the 2.5 per cent inflation target. The European Central Bank, which to some is afflicted by an even greater obsession (it sets its own target, an inflation 'ceiling' of 2 per cent), is according to its critics responsible for Europe's low growth and high unemployment. If only central bankers would loosen up a bit, the argument goes, the economy would do a lot better. Such criticism should not be dismissed out of hand. It is not as if when countries have had significantly higher inflation than now, growth suddenly grinds to a halt. Britain's inflation rate averaged nearly 7.5 per cent during the 1980s and yet the economy enjoyed one of its longest upswings on record, lasting from the spring of 1981 to the summer of 1990. The other question is one of degree. Suppose a central bank is determined to achieve 1 per cent inflation through thick and thin, whether oil prices surge to $100 a barrel or there is some other inflationary shock. Would that be at the expense of growth and jobs? Certainly, although most central bankers would argue that they would never interpret their remit so inflexibly.

The argument that just a little bit more inflation, in normal circumstances, would give us more economic growth dates back to the era of the simple Phillips curve trade-off. Under this, it appeared that there was indeed a choice between unemployment and inflation. As we now know, and as a Labour government discovered as long ago as the 1970s, it does not work like that. Countries that try to buy growth by permitting a little more inflation usually end up with a lot more inflation and little to show for in faster growth. Policies that permit higher inflation may provide a temporary boost – Friedman likened the effects to that of a drug – but eventually make things worse. When expectations enter the equation – people cannot be fooled over and over again – inflationary policies are doomed to failure. In the jargon, there is no long-run trade-off between inflation and growth. Low-inflation economic stability is the best environment for growth. But what is the right inflation rate to aim for? Alan Greenspan, the Federal Reserve Board chairman, defined the right level of inflation as one that does not interfere with economic decisions. At 10 per cent inflation people and businesses start to behave in a way in which at least some of their actions are conditioned by the need to protect themselves against inflation, perhaps by buying index-linked bonds or investing in property. At 2 per cent or 2.5 per cent (the UK target) that is probably not the case. There is also some persuasive evidence, because of the role of expectations, that higher inflation rates are unstable. A country trying to run a 10 per cent inflation target would, according to some research, find itself unable to hold it there, and would face the risk of the disaster of hyperinflation.

All this sounds like carte blanche for the central bankers' club and, indeed, research by Albert Alesina and Larry Summers and others suggests that the more independent the central bank, the better the unemployment–inflation trade-off. With the right policy framework, it seems, you can have it all – low unemployment and low inflation. There is always a risk, though, that central bankers will try a little too hard. Since being given independence in 1997, the Bank of England has tended to undershoot its 2.5 per cent inflation target, despite a requirement that it operate symmetrically around it. Mistakes by the Bank of Japan emanating from excessive worries about inflation helped give the country its deflation of the 1990s, with damaging consequences. Deflation, when the real value of debt increases and monetary policy can become ineffective, is a more dangerous condition than inflation. Why is this? Suppose you take out a mortgage of £100,000 that has to be paid back after twenty-five years. If there is no inflation, then £100,000 is the amount that has to be paid back in real terms. At a 2.5 per cent inflation rate, however, the real value of that debt would halve, so the equivalent of £50,000 would have to be paid back. The knowledge that inflation tends to erode debt's real value is one reason why people and businesses are willing to borrow. Suppose, though, we had deflation – prices falling by 2.5 per cent a year. The real value of the debt would rise, to the equivalent of £200,000, even as the property on which the mortgage was taken out fell in value. In a period of deflation few would want to take on new debts, and defaults would be common. The economy would start to grind to a halt. That is why deflation is to be avoided. Central banks have to be watched closely for this reason alone.

Does manufacturing matter?

Finally, because time is getting on, a perennial question. At a time when three-quarters of the new cars sold in Britain are imported, and the country's factories have long ago ceased to make many of the things sold in our shops, does it matter? Would we be worse off if there was no UK car industry? After all, it does not seem to matter that the big car manufacturers are not British-owned. In other words, does manufacturing matter? The short economic answer to this is no. The decline in manufacturing's share of the economy to under 20 per cent has gone alongside rising, not falling prosperity. Richard Scase has pointed out that more people in Britain work in Indian restaurants than in shipbuilding, steel and coal mining combined, and that there are more public relations consultants than miners. Out of an employed workforce of nearly 30 million, only 4 million are in manufacturing. If Britain's comparative advantage lies elsewhere than in manufacturing, say in tourism or financial services (the City), then the optimal position could be to have no manufacturing industry at all. In fact, there is a long-standing debate between, on one side, those who say the City has never benefited British industry, and those in the Square Mile who say that if only UK manufacturing was as internationally competitive as financial services, the economy would be hugely successful. The arguments for retaining manufacturing become strategic, not economic. Would we really want to have no domestic defence equipment manufacturers? Or, thinking back to the Second World War, would we really, in admittedly very different circumstances, want to be in a position where there would be no domestic manufacturing capacity to convert to producing the modern equivalent of Spitfires?

Real life, of course, is more complicated than that. While manufacturing in Britain is only about a third of the size of the private services sector and a fifth of the economy, it punches above its weight. Manufacturers, for example, contribute more than their fair share of export earnings – manufactured goods account for some 62 per cent of UK exports of goods and services. The economy could not manage without these. Britain has also been successful in attracting inward investment from outside the European Union, particularly Japan and America, much of it into manufacturing. This is hardly the mark of a country that has lost its comparative advantage in making things. Not only that, say advocates of manufacturing, other European countries with larger manufacturing sectors than Britain tend also to have higher living standards, higher per capita GDP. The UK would do better, in other words, with an expanded manufacturing sector. It is also the case, in Britain and elsewhere, that manufacturing firms tend to be more innovative, introducing more technologically driven products and processes than their service-sector counterparts. Innovation, as we have seen, is one of the drivers of economic growth. It may even be that the bald figures understate the importance of manufacturing. The Engineering Employers' Federation and others have pointed out the substantial linkages between industry and other parts of the economy, notably service industries. Without manufacturing as a driver of demand, other parts of the economy would soon suffer. The broad picture is that while it is possible to discuss in the abstract the idea of Britain without a manufacturing sector, the economy will need one for the foreseeable future. That leads on to a further debate: if we need a vibrant and successful manufacturing sector, even a larger one than exists at present, how do we go about creating one? Pretty well every government gets around at some stage to launching a manufacturing strategy. None has yet been notable for its success. A stable economic environment is one essential ingredient, as are a ready supply of skilled workers and a change in the attitudes that have put industry at the bottom of the pecking order when it comes to, for example, graduate career choices. A full answer, however, would require another book.

*
**

It is time to go. We have been here for hours and the waiters are showing their impatience. There are many more arguments we could have about economics and I hope you will have been stimulated to have some. This has been a fairly rich diet of economics and I hope it has not caused any indigestion. I hope too that it has given the lie to the perception that economics is impenetrable and scary. In economics, as in so many things, there is usually nothing to fear except fear itself. Having read this book, nobody need have any fear of economics.

Bite-size glossary

Aggregate demand: Total spending in the economy, or another way of describing gross domestic product. In a closed economy, aggregate demand would consist of spending by consumers and government and on investment (by business and government), as well as any change in stock levels. In an open economy aggregate demand also includes exports, but not imports.

Aggregate supply: The direct counterpart to aggregate demand, being the total of all goods and services produced in an economy over a given period.

Asymmetric shocks: Economic events that affect different countries, or different parts of countries, in distinct ways. It was long thought that Britain would be unable to participate in European economic and monetary union because of sterling's greater sensitivity to oil price changes as a result of

North Sea production.

Automatic stabilizers: If governments allow public spending to rise and tax revenues to fall in a recession without doing anything about it, they are allowing the economy's automatic stabilizers to operate. In a boom, tax revenues could be expected to be strong, public spending weaker.

Average cost: The cost to a firm of producing a product, measured simply by taking the number produced in a given period and dividing it by the total cost. It is distinct from the marginal cost – that of producing an extra unit of output – just as the average rate of income tax, which in Britain is likely to be around 30 per cent even for quite highly paid people, is distinct from the marginal rate of tax, which for top-rate taxpayers is 40 per cent.

Balance of payments: The sum of all a country's transactions with the rest of the world. It builds up from trade in goods, exports and imports, and the trade gap beloved of headline writers, through to the current account. This measures trade in goods and services, as well as the so-called invisible items of trade, such as interest, profit and dividends paid to and received from abroad. The current account is the best overall measure of an economy's external position and whether it is 'paying its way' in the world. The capital account of the balance of payments is made up of long-term investment flows, such as the building of a factory by a foreign firm, portfolio flows, such as investment in stocks and shares in the country, and short-term speculative or 'hot' flows, perhaps attracted by the current interest rate. There are also official flows. A country that has a current account deficit and insufficient capital inflows to match it will probably suffer from a falling exchange rate, it may also have to borrow or run down its foreign exchange reserves. The balance of payments, as its name suggests, has to balance.

Base rate: The interest rate on which the banks base the rates they pay to depositors and charge borrowers. When the Bank of England changes interest rates it is common to refer to a base rate change, although the Bank alters a money-market rate, the so-called 'repo' rate. The base rate is not to be confused with the basic rate, which is the standard rate of income tax.

Bretton Woods: The conference in 1944 that gave birth to the post-war international monetary system, including the International Monetary Fund, the World Bank and the 'gold exchange standard', a system of fixed-but-adjustable exchange rates that lasted until the early 1970s.

Bubble: From the time of the South Sea Bubble of the 1720s, bubble has been used as a term to describe an unsustainable rise in asset prices. Thus, the technology bubble burst in March 2000, while some commentators refer to a house price bubble. The Japanese economy of the late 1980s was subsequently known as the bubble economy.

Budget: The main annual fiscal policy statement, which in Britain is held in March or April and is mainly concerned with tax changes. A Pre-Budget Report, in the autumn, sets out some of the measures beforehand, for consultation. Under current arrangements a Comprehensive Spending

253

Review takes place every two years to agree public spending totals for the following three years.

Budget deficit: What arises when the government's planned spending exceeds the amount it raises in taxation. A budget surplus occurs in the opposite situation, while a balanced budget matches government spending and tax revenues. Governments have adopted various rules over the years to limit their budget deficits. In Britain the Thatcher government ended up with the aim of balancing the budget over the economic cycle, while the Blair Labour government follows the 'golden rule' of borrowing only to fund public investment. Countries inside the euro are required to meet the conditions of the Stability and Growth Pact, limiting their budget deficits to 3 per cent of gross domestic product and in normal circumstances aiming for a balanced budget or small surplus. There are many ways of measuring the budget deficit. For many years the public sector borrowing requirement was the key measure in Britain. Now it has been renamed the public sector net cash requirement, and other measures such as public sector net borrowing have come to prominence.

Business cycle: The tendency to show a regular pattern of faster and slower growth, usually over a four to five year period. The cycle has four phases – recovery, peak, slowdown and trough. When the recovery is particularly strong it becomes a boom, when the slowdown is sharp it may turn into a 'bust' or recession. Governments and central banks often try to dampen the effects of the cycle by using fiscal and monetary policy. Real business cycle theorists such as Robert

Lucas advise against this. There are plenty of other types of business cycle. A Juglar cycle, after the French economist Clement Juglar, lasts nine to ten years. A Kondratiev cycle, after the Russian economist Nikolai Kondratiev, lasts around fifty years. There is considerable debate about the continued existence of all these cycles. In the 1980s the UK Chancellor Nigel Lawson claimed to have abolished the business cycle.

Capital expenditure: Investment by companies or governments in plant, machinery, vehicles, buildings, or, in the case of governments, the infrastructure.

Central bank: The institution responsible for monetary policy and in some countries (not Britain) financial and banking regulation. The Bank of England, the European Central Bank, the Federal Reserve Board and the Bank of Japan are the world's major central banks.

Comparative advantage: The theory, developed by David Ricardo, in which countries can benefit from trade even if one has an absolute advantage in the production of all goods and services.

Competition policy: Measures taken by governments to break down monopolies or other dominant positions within markets by firms, thus encouraging competition. In Britain since 1997 the Office of Fair Trading has been given an enhanced role in investigating and recommending action against anti-competitive behaviour, while the Competition Commission, which polices monopolies, has effectively been given independence from government. It used to be thought that there were 'public interest' monopolies – companies that were dominant in the home market but could use this as a spring-board in the world market. Such thinking, that a monopoly position for national champions should be permitted, is no longer fashionable.

Competitiveness: Essentially the ability of a country or its exports to compete internationally. Some economists argue that it is appropriate to measure competitiveness only among companies, not countries. Even so, a country that is uncompetitive will probably run a current account deficit, and may need a lower exchange rate, as well as more fundamental corrective measures.

Crowding out: The situation in which an increase in government activity results in a fall in private sector activity, either because the public sector lays claim on resources (particularly workers) that could have been used by private firms, or because increased government borrowing pushes up interest rates.

Current expenditure: Expenditure on non-capital items. Spending by governments on the wages and salaries of public sector workers, or on schoolbooks and medicines, all comes under the heading of current expenditure.

Deflation: A fall in the general price level, the opposite of inflation. The last global deflationary episode was in the 1930s, although Japan also experienced deflation in the 1990s. Reference is sometimes made to deflationary policies. These are not aimed at bringing about deflation but, rather, slowing a strongly growing economy. A central bank raising interest rates or a government increasing taxes or cutting public spending could be said to be introducing deflationary policies.

Depreciation: Two distinct meanings, the first being the declining value of a capital asset due to wear and tear and obsolescence. The second is the right expression for a fall in the value of a currency during an era of floating rates. If the pound falls from $1.60 to $1.40 against the dollar, it has depreciated.

Depression: A prolonged economic downturn or period of stagnation, as distinct from a shorter recession. The last worldwide depression was in the 1930s.

Devaluation: The correct expression for a fall in the value of a currency during a fixed rate era, such as the Bretton Woods system that lasted from just after the Second World War until 1973. In November 1967 the pound was devalued from $2.80 to $2.40 against the dollar, remaining at the new lower level.

Diminishing returns: The situation in which a firm applies additional factors of production, for example extra workers, to increasing output but achieves a smaller increase in output for every additional worker employed. Diminishing marginal utility refers to the declining satisfaction each additional unit of consumption brings – one whisky might be enjoyable, the tenth much less so.

Direct taxation: Taxes on income, for example income tax or National Insurance contributions, or in the case of companies, corporation tax.

Disinflation: A reduction in the rate of inflation, not to be confused with deflation, a fall in prices.

Disposable income: Income after (direct) tax.

Econometrics: The application of mathematical and statistical techniques to economic theories and relationships. The equations that make up models of the economy are estimated using econometric techniques.

Economic growth: The rise in gross domestic product, or per capita GDP, from one year to the next. Growth is the ultimate aim of economic policy. The trend rate of economic growth in Britain, its average over time, is currently estimated by the Treasury to be 2.75 per cent.

Efficient market hypothesis: The theory that the level of the stock market, or any other financial market, reflects the efficient use by market participants of all the information available to them.

Elasticity of demand: The responsiveness of demand for a product to a change in its price, or to a change in the incomes of consumers.

Euroland: Popular name for the area covered by European economic and monetary union, the euro area. Euroland came into being on 1 January 1999 with eleven members (Austria, Belgium, Finland, France, Germany, Ireland, Italy, Luxembourg, the Netherlands, Portugal and Spain). Greece joined later.

Exchange rate: The value of one currency, expressed in terms of another, for example the pound's exchange rate against the dollar is $1.50.

Externalities: Costs, or benefits, generated by firms or individuals but affecting others. Pollution is a common negative externality, which is why firms are subject to anti-pollution controls and penalties. An attractive garden might generate positive externalities – benefiting not only its owner but also passers-by.

Fiscal policy: Strictly speaking, matters pertaining to tax. The fiscal year is the tax year. In practice, fiscal policy refers to the tax and spending decisions by governments, usually taken annually in Budgets. The role of fiscal policy has changed over the years. In the 1950s and 1960s it was used for 'fine-tuning' purposes – managing demand in the economy. Now fiscal policy is usually framed in a medium-term context, with tax changes seen as impacting on economic performance and public spending also usually planned for some years in advance. Fiscal drag is a technical term describing the fact that in the absence of changes, the tax government takes from individuals will normally rise as a result of inflation as rising incomes move people into higher tax brackets. This is why income tax allowances, for example, are conventionally raised in line with inflation.

Floating currencies: The system that has existed since the early 1970s, in which currencies are not fixed in value against others. The dollar, the yen, the euro and the pound float freely. Not all currencies are floating. Some are tied to the dollar while European currencies were linked in the exchange rate mechanism of the European Monetary System prior to the adoption of the euro.

Full employment: In practice, an unemployment rate of 2 or 3 per cent – when everybody who could reasonably be in work is in employment. Why not zero? Because there will always be some people moving between jobs (frictional unemployment) and temporarily unemployed because of the weather or the state of the tourist trade (seasonal unemployment). Employment may still rise in a situation of full employment if more people can be lured into the workforce, for example married women or older people.

Game theory: The modelling of economic decision-making by means of games or strategies. Outcomes for firms and individuals depend not only on their decisions and strategies but also on what others do. The pioneers of game theory were John Von Neumann and Oskar Morgenstern, in their 1944 *Theory of Games and Economic Behaviour.* They gave us the idea of the 'zero sum game' in which one player's gain is another's loss. John Nash was responsible for demonstrating that the outcome of a game, in other words of any economic decision, could be a 'win–win' one.

Gini coefficient: The standard measure of inequality within or between countries. It varies between 0 and 1. A Gini coefficient of 0 would imply a perfectly equal distribution of income, with everybody getting the same, while a coefficient of 1 would mean that one person would receive everything.

Gold standard: The international monetary system in which all currencies were fully backed by and convertible into gold.

Golden rule: A self-imposed fiscal rule that says the government should borrow only for investment, not current spending.

Government bonds: Interest-bearing bonds issued by the government to borrow from the financial markets or the public.

Bonds are of short- (up to five years), medium-, or long-term duration – up to thirty years, sometimes longer. The yield, or interest, on government bonds is an important determinant of interest rates elsewhere in the economy. In Britain government bonds are called gilts (gilt-edged securities).

Gross domestic product: GDP, the most common measure of overall activity in the economy within a given period. GDP can be calculated three ways – it is the total of spending (GDP = C + I + G + X − M), the sum of production, and the total of all incomes received. All three should produce roughly the same answer. GDP at market prices includes taxation, while GDP adjusted for taxes and subsidies is GDP at factor cost. Gross national product is roughly similar to GDP, but also includes net property income from abroad. In some countries the GDP/GNP difference is quite significant, but not in the case of Britain.

Group of Seven: A grouping of the world's most powerful countries, the G7 started life as the Group of Five (America, Japan, Britain, Germany and France) in the mid-1970s, with Canada and Italy added soon afterwards. The G7, which now includes Russia at some of its meetings, when it becomes the G8, holds annual summits and more frequent meetings between its finance ministers and central bankers.

Human capital: Without a skilled and educated workforce, investment in the latest machinery will be futile. Investing in human capital, in education and training, can be as important as investing in equipment, although the returns may take longer to show through.

Hyperinflation: Runaway inflation, when the value of money falls at an alarming rate. Countries with inflation rates of 50 per cent or more *per month* are experiencing hyperinflation.

Indifference curve: A representation of a consumer's preferences between apples and pears, or income and leisure, or anything else. A consumer may be indifferent between five apples and five pears, or three apples and eight pears, and so on. Indifference curves can never cross.

Indirect taxation: Mainly taxes on spending, such as VAT and excise duties.

Inflation: A general increase in the price level, and one of the main targets for modern-day economic policy. The UK inflation target of 2.5 per cent sounds low but it means prices would double in just over twenty-five years. A 4 per cent target would mean a doubling of prices every fifteen years. Economists regard a small amount of inflation as desirable, not least to avoid the danger of deflation. Strictly speaking, inflation should be used only to measure a general increase in prices but people often refer to house price inflation or wage inflation. The main measure of inflation used in Britain is based on the retail prices index, although producer price inflation data (industry's input and output costs) are also published. The most comprehensive inflation measure is derived from GDP data, the GDP deflator.

Infrastructure: Roads, railways, telecommunications, hospitals, schools and other forms of public investment, these are usually but not necessarily built and maintained by government. An inadequate infrastructure has been blamed for undermining Britain's economic performance.

Interest rate: The cost of borrowing, or the price of money. The amount that has to be paid to a lender for foregoing the use of money now. The rate of interest, more importantly, is the main weapon of monetary policy. Raising interest rates – increasing the cost of borrowing – tightens policy, and vice versa.

J-curve: A description of the likely balance of payments effects of currency devaluation. Initially the current account worsens, because imports have become more expensive. Only later is there an improvement as exports benefit from the devaluation.

Keynesian policies: The use of a fiscal policy in an activist way to manage demand in the economy. A recession would be tackled with higher public spending and tax cuts, and the opposite policies would be adopted in a boom. The heyday of Keynesian policies was in the 1950s and 1960s.

Laffer curve: A graphical demonstration of the fact that higher tax rates can result in lower tax revenues.

Liquidity trap: The situation, defined by Keynes, in which monetary policy becomes ineffective because interest rates cannot fall low enough to stimulate economic activity. When there is deflation or falling prices, there is also likely to be a liquidity trap.

Marginal rate of tax: The tax paid on an additional pound of income earned. A higher rate taxpayer in Britain pays a marginal tax rate of 40 per cent. Marginal cost, marginal revenue and marginal utility are all key concepts in economics. Firms produce to the point where marginal cost equals marginal revenue. In each case 'marginal' refers to an additional unit.

Monetarism: The belief that inflation is 'always and everywhere' a monetary phenomenon and that inflation results from increases in the money supply. While agreeing on this general position, monetarists argue among themselves about the choice of target measures for the money supply and about how best to control them. The modern heyday for monetarism was in the 1980s.

Monetary policy: Decisions that affect the cost and availability of money. Monetary policy, mainly exercised through interest rate changes, is regarded as the most effective tool for short-term economic management.

Monetary policy committee: A committee within the Bank of England of nine men and women that meets each month to agree the level of interest rates. The MPC, which is chaired by the governor of the Bank, came into being in 1997 when the Bank was given 'operational independence', control over interest rates. It is charged with achieving an inflation target set by the government, currently 2.5 per cent. Five members of the committee are Bank 'insiders', including the governor and two deputies; four are outside appointments, made by the Chancellor of the Exchequer.

Money supply: The stock of money is the amount of money in circulation; the money supply describes changes in that stock in a given period. Measures of the money stock (and money supply) range from the very narrow such as M0, mainly notes and coin, to the very broad, M5, which includes all forms of credit and deposits.

Monopoly: Strictly speaking a situation in which there is only one firm in an industry. A monopsony refers to a single buyer for an industry's products. In practice, monopoly situations develop when a firm establishes a dominant position within an industry. Oligopoly refers to dominance of an industry by a few large players, as is the case for Britain's supermarkets and banks.

Multiplier: Essential to Keynesian economics, the notion that an injection of spending has knock-on effects beyond the initial impact. An extra £5 billion of government spending will, in creating incomes for public sector workers and suppliers, create additional spending elsewhere in the economy. Keynesians have traditionally argued that these multiplier effects are large, while post-Keynesian economists say they will be neutralized by the fact that people will recognize that higher government spending will result either in future tax rises or inflation.

Natural rate of unemployment, Nairu: The level of unemployment consistent with a stable rate of inflation. The Nairu, another way of describing the natural rate, is the non-accelerating inflation rate of unemployment. The idea, introduced by Milton Friedman, is that the natural rate is determined by supply-side factors, such as the skills of the workforce and how they are distributed around the country, together with factors such as the operation of the benefits system (over-generous benefits discourage the low-paid from taking jobs). Measures to expand the economy and reduce unemployment below the natural rate will result in inflation. Most economists accept the existence of a natural rate or Nairu, although they have found it difficult to estimate exactly where it is at any one time, making it an imprecise tool for policymakers.

Optimal currency area: An area or group of countries in which it is appropriate to have a single currency, this concept has been much used in the debate over the euro.

Output gap: A broad measure of spare capacity in the economy, the difference between actual GDP and its trend or long-run level. An economy which starts on trend, and has a trend rate of growth of 2.5 per cent, would have a positive output gap (i.e. spare capacity) after two years of 1 per cent growth, but a negative output gap – it would be operating above capacity – after two years of 4 per cent growth. Again, it would be a more useful tool for policymakers if economists were better at estimating it.

Perfect competition: The textbook model of a market, with many firms producing identical products and each having to accept the same market price for their product. Buyers have perfect information. For a time, some economists believed the Internet had characteristics of perfect competition.

Phillips curve: The relationship between unemployment and wage inflation developed by A. W. 'Bill' Phillips. The higher the level of unemployment, the lower the rate of wage inflation. In the late 1960s Milton Friedman introduced a new version of the Phillips curve, adjusted for expectations about inflation.

Productivity: An important determinant of prosperity. Labour productivity is output divided by the number of workers (or worker-hours) needed to produce it. The faster the rate of growth in productivity over time, the higher the trend rate of growth of GDP. Capital productivity is the same concept applied to investment. Total factor productivity is the combination of labour and capital productivity.

Quantity theory of money: The formal basis of monetarism, the link between the money supply and inflation. $MV = PT$ (or PY), where M is the money stock, V its velocity of circulation, P the price level, T the number of transactions (Y is real GDP). Changes in M, money, will mostly be reflected in changes in P, prices.

Rational expectations: The important concept that says economic actors (people and businesses) learn from the past – they do not make the same mistake twice. Most associated with George Lucas, it demonstrated for example that governments would be unable to fool the public with an inflationary burst of extra state spending.

Real interest rate: The rate of interest adjusted for inflation. A depositor getting 5 per cent interest at a time of 2 per cent inflation is doing better than one earning 10 per cent interest when inflation is 8 per cent.

Real terms: Any economic variable adjusted for price changes, or inflation. Without such adjustments, comparisons would be meaningless. A 20 per cent rise in actual or 'nominal' GDP at a time of 20 per cent inflation represents zero real growth, while a 3 per cent rise at a time of 1 per cent inflation is equivalent to 2 per cent real growth.

Recession: Usually defined as two consecutive quarters of falling GDP, although it can apply to any pronounced slow-down. The National Bureau of Economic Research in America, the official recession arbiter, said the US economy experienced a recession in 2001–2 even though GDP did not fall for two successive quarters.

Saving ratio: The proportion of income saved during a given period. Traditionally, countries such as Japan have had a high saving ratio, while Britain and America have had low saving ratios. In a closed economy, the amount of saving would determine the funds available for investment, although that is not the case where capital flows freely. Saving is usually divided into its discretionary (deliberate decisions to save) and non-discretionary (such as automatic pension contributions) components. Saving is also a net variable, so heavy borrowing by individuals will reduce the saving ratio.

Seasonal adjustment: Any economic variable adjusted for seasonal variations. Many indicators are adjusted in this way to allow meaningful comparisons between different times of year. Without such adjustment there would always be an apparent surge in consumer spending growth in November and December in anticipation of Christmas. Economists need to know how much of that surge is normal.

Supply-side economics: The branch of economics concerned with the factors that raise or lower the economy's long-run or trend growth rate. In the 1980s the 'supply-siders', mainly free market economists in America, were concerned with matters such as tax cuts to restore incentives and deregulation to improve the workings of markets. Today, supply-side economics would be regarded as much wider than that, taking in the role of education and training, and 'active' labour market measures to encourage greater participation in the job market.

Symmetric target: A target in which the penalties for undershooting are identical (symmetrical) to those for overshooting. The Bank of England's 2.5 per cent inflation target is symmetrical. If inflation falls below 1.5 per cent or rises above 3.5 per cent, the governor of the Bank of England has to write a letter of explanation to the Chancellor.

Tax credits: A form of payment by government to individuals or firms that normally reduces the amount of tax payable. Tax credits also often result in a net payment by the tax authorities to the non-tax-paying recipient.

Transfer payments: That part of government spending that consists of a transfer from taxpayers to benefit recipients, for example state pensioners or the unemployed.

Underlying inflation: A measure of inflation adjusted for special or temporary factors. The target measure of inflation used in Britain, the retail prices index excluding mortgage interest payments, is an underlying measure. The target rate is 2.5 per cent. One rationale for excluding mortgage payments is that otherwise action by the Bank of England to reduce inflation, raising interest rates, would have the short-term effect of pushing inflation higher.

Unemployment rate: The percentage of eligible people who are not in work. Not as easy as it sounds. In Britain one measure of eligibility (the claimant count) is based on entitlement to benefit, the jobseekers' allowance, while another, the

International Labour Office measure, counts all those who want to work, whether entitled to benefit or not.

Wealth: The stock of assets owned by, say, an individual, as distinct from income, which is the flow of money coming in each year. To the extent it is not spent, income adds to wealth.

Post-prandial reading

Economics, as I hope this book has demonstrated, is a living subject. There is a wealth of information, much of it good, in the newspapers, including of course the *Sunday Times*, www.sunday-times.co.uk, *The Times*, www.the-times.co.uk, the *Financial Times*, www.ft.com and the *Guardian*, www.guardian.co.uk, and in weekly magazines such as the *Economist*, www.economist.com, subscription-only at the time of writing. The Internet is also a wonderful source including, in Britain, the Bank of England, www.bankofengland.co.uk, the Treasury, www.hm-treasury.gov.uk, the Office for National Statistics, www.statistics.gov.uk and organizations such as the Institute for Fiscal Studies, www.ifs.org.uk, the Royal Economic Society, www.res.org.uk, as well as my own site, www.economicsuk.com. Internationally, the Organisation for Economic Co-operation and Development, www.oecd.org, the

International Monetary Fund, www.imf.org, the European Central Bank, www.ecb.int and America's www.economy.com are all excellent resources.

There is a generous supply of books on economics, some of them very good, some quite hard work. Rather than litter this book with references, which serve only to clutter up the text, I decided to keep some recommendations until the end, which include those works I have referred to. Starting with the history of economic thought, readers have quite a choice. William Barber's *A History of Economic Thought* (Penguin) is accessible, while Paul Strathern's *Dr Strangelove's Game, A Brief History of Economic Genius* (Hamish Hamilton) is quirky, informative and entertaining. *The Making of Modern Economics* by Mark Skousen (M. E. Sharpe) is full of anecdote, photographs of the great economists – and some of the not so great – and has a wonderfully light touch. Harder, but useful for serious students are Eric Roll's *A History of Economic Thought* (Faber & Faber) and Mark Blaug's *The History of Economic Thought* (Edward Elgar).

The lives of the great economists, as well as their original works, always repay reading. Various edited paperback versions of Adam Smith's *The Wealth of Nations* are in print, including one from Penguin, while Ian Simpson Ross's *The Life of Adam Smith* (Clarendon Press) tells the story of Smith's life. John Maynard Keynes merited a three-volume biography, by Robert Skidelsky: volume one is *Hopes Betrayed, 1883–1920*, volume two is *The Economist as Saviour, 1920–37*, and the final volume is *Fighting for Britain, 1937–46*. All are published by Macmillan. Keynes's *The General Theory of Employment, Interest and Money*

POST-PRANDIAL READING

(Prometheus Books) is in print. Two other biographies are worth mentioning: Francis Wheen's *Karl Marx* (Fourth Estate) is a good read as, coming up to date, is Sylvia Nasar's story of the remarkable life of John Nash, *A Beautiful Mind* (Faber & Faber).

The route to economic understanding is often through economic history. Eric Hobsbawm's *Industry and Empire* (Penguin), an economic history of Britain, has always been a favourite of mine. *Sterling, the Rise and Fall of a Currency* (Penguin), by Nicholas Mayhew, tells the pound's often inglorious story. On a grander scale, *The Wealth and Poverty of Nations* by David Landes (Abacus) is excellent. As for modern UK economic history, Geoffrey Owen's *From Empire to Europe* (HarperCollins) describes post-war British economy from an industrial perspective. Two books of mine, *The Rise and Fall of Monetarism* and *From Boom to Bust*, both originally published by Penguin, do so from the perspective of economic policy. Anybody who has difficulty obtaining these should contact me and we will try to get a reprint organized. The policy perspective on economics has also been provided by some of those who have witnessed it at first hand. Nigel Lawson's *The View from No.11* (Corgi) is a great account of the Thatcher years and of how economic policy works in practice. Coming right up to date, *Reforming Britain's Economic and Financial Policy* (Palgrave), written by the Treasury and edited by Ed Balls and Gus O'Donnell, Gordon Brown's most senior lieutenants, is an account of economic policy changes since 1997. A fun account of different Chancellors since 1945 is provided by Richard Holt in *Second Among Equals* (Profile Books). David Lipsey's *The Secret Treasury*

273

(Viking) is informative, but in a more buttoned-up way.

On the subject of policy, *Both Sides of the Coin*, by James Forder and Christopher Huhne (Profile Books), is a good example of two economists engaged in debate on a key issue, UK membership of the euro. My own *Will Europe Work?* (Profile Books) looks at the euro issue from the perspective of optimal currency areas.

Economists who write accessibly are still in short supply, particularly in Britain. We do not have a British Paul Krugman, whose books *Peddling Prosperity* (W. W. Norton) and *The Accidental Theorist* (Penguin) debunk from a position of great knowledge. I also like Steven Landsburg's *The Armchair Economist* (Simon & Schuster).

Students of economics are used to bulky tomes which could easily be sold by weight. Samuelson's *Economics* (McGraw-Hill) is still in print, the latest edition being co-written with William Nordhaus. *Economics* (McGraw-Hill) by David Begg, Stanley Fischer and Rudiger Dornbusch is a set text on many courses. A relatively new book, *Macroeconomics, Understanding the Wealth of Nations* (John Wiley & Sons), by David Miles and Andrew Scott, is rather good. Many of the existing textbooks will be given a run for their money by a new one, *Principles of Economics*, by Paul Krugman and Robin Wells, published by Worth.

Acknowledgements

This book is the result of conversations, arguments and lunches over many years, with economists too numerous to mention. Their help, and, going back a little further, that of my teachers, is gratefully acknowledged. It is often, in addition, the questions and comments of non-economists, particularly readers, that make you think and encourage delving into new areas. As always, I am grateful for this dialogue, these days mainly via e-mail. At Profile Books, my thanks to Andrew Franklin, Kate Griffin and their colleagues for their help and support. Andrew and I first worked together on a book nearly two decades ago, and he is as energetic and enthusiastic now as he was then. At home, my thanks as always to Jane, Richard, Thomas, Emily and Elizabeth. I hope, in return, this book is of some help to them.

Index